What Is My Purpose IN LIFE?

BOB KING

CONTENTS

What is My Purpose of My Life?

SUBTITLES:

➲ Where does it begin?

➲ The Secular Life and the Religious or Spiritual Life.

The title of this book is, 'What is the purpose of my life?'
Let me be clear from the beginning that I DO have a purpose in my life and as a result of that I am a fairly happy man. I chose this topic for my book because I read a lot of psychology books and philosophy books by people who expound upon the general state of happiness in the world, or perhaps more so, the state of unhappiness.

Most of the commentators state that there is a lot of unhappiness in the world and that comes mainly because many people cannot see a purpose in their lives or cannot find any meaning in it. That is understandable when we look at the crazy things that are going on in the world at this time.

Like I said, I am a happy man. Thus, why would I use a title like that for my book that could be interpreted as someone who is wallowing in self-pity? THAT IS NOT THE CASE. I use it only because I know that there are many unhappy people out there who often ask that question and many of those people are desperate for an answer. They may have felt good about life at one time, but they no longer do. Such a state may be sad, and in extreme cases, it might be even tragic, but I say, read on. Let us look at some options, both personal ones and spiritual ones.

Because I have had many experiences in my life as a musician, author, and a teacher, these are the topics that I like to write about. I am a Christian, so I know my writing may be biased, but that doesn't really matter because the skepticism about my religion is superseded by the true principles that are actually found there and by the clinical evidence that is found by people who conduct surveys on the happiness quotient in the general population, be they religious or non religious people. I like to probe for information from anyone who is willing to give it on this very serious topic. I continually seek for useable truth and for confirmation that my theological ideas are valid ones.

Thus, if there are any positive ideas I can spread around to 'joy challenged people'. I am excited to do so, and grateful for that opportunity. The counsel that I give might not be to everyone's way of thinking at first, but that is alright because I am certain that my average reader will be able to pick up on a few things here and there that strike a chord with them, even some things that might make a difference in their lives.

If so, those things might just add up and the next thing you know, your friends will have a walking 'dynamo' on their hands. In fact, I once wrote a song entitled 'Attitudes can be Contagious'. It's a true principle.

Where does it begin?

We must begin with gaining an understanding of a very important principle. It happens to be more of a theological principal than a philosophical principal. This principle is given to us by our Heavenly Father in scripture, and It goes like this.

> *"For the natural man is an enemy to God and has been from the fall of Adam, and will be forever and ever, unless he yields to the enticings of the Holy Spirit and putteth off the natural man and becometh a saint through the Atonement of Christ the Lord."*
>
> *– Mosiah 3: 19 (Book of Mormon)*

This statement is not a reason for human beings to feel bad or feel like they are unworthy creatures. In reality, it should make us feel good because God has 'revealed' to us a pivotal principal. He wants us to know that even though all men and women all men and women need God to assist them and teach them. The human beings themselves must contribute <u>something</u> to the plan. Otherwise, they would be under no obligation, and thus the notion of a 'joint effort' will probably be discarded by them. Thus, it says in the above scripture says that we must rise above our natural state and work towards a better one and get to the point where our inner soul is ready to accept and even embrace accept that higher state (as long as it makes sense). I say this because, aside from being a believer in the power of the human spirit, I am also a rationalist.

I am not a science denier, but the field of science from what I have read is inly interested in the material data, or 'seen data', that can further a strong diagnosis. Science holds no faith in unseen data. I believe that happiness, of any kind, is first triggered by the spirit, and then it spreads to the body, the heart, and the mind. I therefore I think that if we neglect the inner feelings of our soul in our lives, we will depriving ourselves of an essential ingredient that will help us to overcome our distractions and our anxieties. If we can tap into our spirit on a spiritual/mental/physical level, we will find ourselves becoming slowly happier and healthier.

This 'rational' philosophy of mine, which includes the unseen spirit, is a part of the 'Plan of Happiness'. For people who have no concept of a God or Creator, this also involves another principle. That is the principle of 'honest self analysis', which should cause us all to ask questions about our purpose in life itself. To begin that part of the journey a person must realize that, if they look around and they are living with no knowledge of a benevolent Creator, then something will be missing in their lives. It will be quite appropriate then to ask questions of God in prayer and humility.

"And I say unto you, Ask and it shall be given you; seek and ye shall find; knock, and it shall be opened unto you." - Luke 11:9

Once you receive your answer, then that will be where making covenants comes in. God's people must be a 'covenant making' people. That makes them complicit in the deal, and possibly even co-creators by 'squaring everything off'. Ask yourself then 'do you feel gratitude for being asked to participate in a Holy endeavor?' You may not feel that way now, but in time, after you learn all the true factors that are involved in the plan, I suspect that you will feel grateful. We should feel privileged that our Heavenly Father has chosen us to help Him accomplish His Heavenly, and Eternal goals.

The essays I write that have a spiritual or religious context will supply you with some information that you may not know about if you have never taken the time to study it out thoroughly. This is in the hope that it might give you some new perspectives, if need be, and in doing so it may even change your priorities, if need be.

The Secular Life and the Religious Life

There are two basic theories about the nature of our lives. One theory is the religious theory, which amounts to a life with a God, or Creator, or a Heavenly Father, or an intelligent designer who is at the helm of it. The other theory is the secular theory, which says that there is no God at the helm. What you see is what you get. What you see as the purpose of your life will very much depend upon which theory you adhere to.

Thus, as I talk about the purpose of life in this chapter my focus will be twofold. The first 'fold' will be concerned with the purpose of <u>a secular life</u>. That is a life without religion and without a God. So I ask, is there really any meaning or purpose in such a life? The answer to that question, for me, is fairly straightforward and I will give it to you right off the bat. It goes like this. The answer to finding lasting meaning or happiness in a secular life is simply that **a person cannot do it**.

The Preacher in the book of Ecclesiastes lived a secular life for a time and this is how he summed it up:

> *"Vanity of vanities, saith the Preacher. All is vanity."*
> *- Ecclesiastes 1: 2*

If a man or a woman thinks they can find happiness without any connection to the Creator of all happiness, I would say that they are mistaken and they are travelling in a land of illusion and a land of narcissism. It is a land of materialistic people, including accusers, alcoholics and drug addicts and people who have, tragically, fallen away from the straight and narrow path.

As I said in a previous book, ('Life Goes On And On') there are two main reasons why life's purpose seems to be unclear to some people. The first clue in finding purpose, meaning and happiness is finding that often elusive state of <u>joy</u> and the second clue is to learn how to keep it.

By saying 'keeping it' I am referring here to a state of <u>permanence</u>. That is the second thing that all people will need in order to find true happiness. Without permanence, a joyful state will end one day and come to a close, so what good was it then we will ask, apart from a few good memories that will soon fade into nothingness as our physical reference points slowly disintegrate?

When we consider this notion we must consider that, without God we are just like sheep, that is, sheep who have no shepherd to be with us to give us proper instructions and teach us a proper way whereby we can achieve happiness and prosperity.

To study purpose, a person must first have to become familiar with joy, and even different kinds of joy. Let it be noticed that the word 'joy' here could have a substitute, like 'peace', or 'contentment' or 'satisfaction'. Again, a secular mindset that can provide temporary joy, or peace, to a man or woman, but could not sustain a spirit of joy over time unless permanence was granted to it.

Such a state of permanence, even after we die, could only be given to us by our 'Creator' who is the 'author of life' and who was also the author of all kinds of joy. He is also our Heavenly father who loves us. That is why our Spiritual parents created us. He desires that His children prepare to receive permanence, or 'Eternal life' for the simple reason that our Creator is eternal or 'permanent' and once we learn this fact, then it makes sense that we should attempt to follow in the path that He has laid out for us. If a soul is not prepared for this permanence, or Eternal life, then all bets are off, so to speak.

God knows this and that is why he has gone to great lengths to send us good and thorough instructions. There still may be some guesswork involved, but the effectiveness of that depends upon our willingness to obey those instructions as exactly as we can, and to be diligent in achieving righteous goals. Those instructions can also be found through personal prayer and found within the writings in Holy Scriptures, and in the words of prophets past and present.

Regarding joy, if one's final state was a permanent one, but had no joy within it, then who would want to live there? Personally, I desire permanence. I desire to achieve Eternal life in an eternal, and a happy realm, where I am protected from all kinds of temptation or harm. It would be difficult for me to imagine myself abandoning that great desire of mine for any reason. Thus, the context and conditions of my chosen state of eternal rest will always be worth embracing and contemplating and striving to attain.

How can a person attain a joyful and permanent state like that? Read on. The first part of the deal though has already been stated. For anyone to find happiness, we will require joy, or 'peace' or 'satisfaction', or 'contentment'. But we will also need permanence.

The status of our final state would be mostly due to the decisions that we make in our mortal lives not because it is a law, but because those are the things that will shape our characters.

It is a fact and a true blessing from God that what we have all been granted involves our freedom to choose principles that we will adopt and embrace in our daily lives. Our mortal life is a probationary period that we spend living on our often beautiful, but often precarious planet, where our initial time is spent. That planet is also known as the planet 'Earth'.

One might ask if we, as fallible human beings, should err in our judgments, is it not possible for God to come down and instruct us in the proper ways of learning so that we might be able to correct any mistakes we might have made and thus, correct our course? Yes, it is possible, but I don't know if it would be expedient for Him to do that. That is because that process can sometimes be a long and complicated one. As it happens, simple human beings are not always willing to learn principles from what we are told is an ultimate authority who we do not know very well. Thus, we only have one alternative. We must come to know Him, in a spiritual sense, not in a physical sense.

Therefore, I think it is likely that God would <u>not</u> necessarily instruct us on a one on one basis, because that would bring in the intimidation factor and His divine teaching and our learning would be reduced to a process of simply <u>obeying orders</u>. The life process has much more to offer than that.

Thus, God has given His word to ALL people so that each one if us will have a chance to follow Him in His path and there will be no special circumstances for any of us. We will all have a choice as to which basic plan we will follow. By the way, the fact that there will be no special circumstances for any of us has been illustrated by the fact that God, Himself, as He allowed the painful torture and execution of His beloved and only begotten Son, Jesus Christ.

God is a wise teacher and He knows that a certain amount of work, and even suffering, is sometimes necessary to teach His students about harsh consequences that come from travelling on the 'wrong' path. I cannot speak for Him, but it makes sense to me, and I am very sincere about it, so please take it for what you think it is worth.

I think that God probably knows that the most effective way of learning comes from comes from within the students themselves, assuming that they are given some guidance, both in spiritual ways and in practical ways. Thus, in a spiritual way, people en masse will be given churches (ones that genuinely seek the truth being the preferred ones) and knowledge of spiritual gifts that they might use. I speak here about prophets, apostles, and divinely inspired scriptures. We also have the example of Jesus Christ, and the direct influence of the Holy Ghost who lives within people and can often speak to the people in His own way.

The actual teaching of truthful principles comes by, what I call 'a spark of inspiration. That spark is God-sent to us and usually comes to us by the Spirit of the Holy Ghost. We never really know when He is going to bestow that on us. Thus, we must always be on the lookout for it.

The teaching of truthful principles are best taught by the originator, or originators, of those principles. The givers of that gift, therefore, must have ultimate knowledge and be virtuous, compassionate, powerful and yet humble. Truly Divine Beings must be mighty beings, who have proven those qualities in the past. Our God, I would think, is the only one who could fulfill those requirements. I also believe that God has angels who can teach many of the gospel principles with authority, both in this life and in the after-life realms.

The Religious or Spiritual Life

This leads us to the second question. Can a person find happiness in a spiritual or a religious life? I say that they most definitely can and that is where God Himself comes in. A person can find happiness and meaning in a religious life and the reason for that is because, by the grace of God, permanence can be allowed into any person's realm as long as that person desires it and asks for it and who, as well, can handle it intellectually, physically and morally.

That is what the Lord's plan of happiness is all about. That might seem impossible, but we are made in His likeness, and if He did not think we could do it, I am sure that He would not give us the obligation to do so.

I am writing specifically here about Christianity because that is the religion that says the most about an afterlife that exists in a heavenly realm where anyone can go to as long as they are willing to accept God and accept the conditions that exist there in Heaven.

Do I preach because I feel that I am morally superior to other people? No. I preach for two reasons. One is because I like talking about ultimate things in life and speculating on the nature of what will happen in the next life too. After much study I have discovered that there is more to that future world than meets the eye. In my church I have been ordained a minister and so I have a calling to assist others in their lives and to spread the gospel of Jesus Christ to those who might be in need of it, even those in desperate need of it. In the bible such a calling is mentioned fairly early in the book of Isaiah:

"The Spirit of the Lord God is upon me; because the Lord hath appointed me to preach good tidings unto the meek; he hath sent me to bind up the broken hearted, to proclaim liberty to the captives, and the opening of the prison to them who are bound."

- Isaiah 61:1

The word 'Reverend' which I sometimes use, means, according to the dictionary, 'a member of the clergy' which I am in my church. Thus, I like to discuss the nature of Divinity and its implications. As well, I always leave a space during my talks for anyone to ask any questions.

Let me be clear that I use the pronoun 'He' to refer to God in this book, but in my book 'Realms I have known, I also introduce a female God, or Goddess, who is equal to the Father. But for reasons that I explain in the book, she is shrouded in anonymity for her own protection. In any case this will clear up any feminist notions that my religion is male-based.

I think that a spiritual Creator needs to be a spiritual 'person' at some level. Does not the Bible say that we were created in His image? From my readings in the scriptures I could also say that this God/person is our spiritual 'Father'. He is a God who is loving and wise, and who has power over the elements of this world that He has created. This spiritual being is also one who lives in an Endless period of time and recognizes that. His Spirit, like all spirits, is permanent. Because our human spirits are new at this 'mortal life thing', our progress will be based mostly on merit.

Here is another principal about God that I think is worth considering. Despite what some people say, I think that there is no such thing as 'unconditional' love. The term is not mentioned in the scriptures and that would displace the whole idea of wisdom, and God would not do that. The whole idea of Heaven and Hell, or even various levels of heaven, is based upon 'conditions'.

> *"The glory of God is intelligence, or in other words, light and truth."*
>
> *- Doctrine and Covenants 93: 36*

That means that a person needs to prove themselves to be worthy of a high station according to their righteous desires and the evidence of the good acts that they have performed while they lived in the mortal realm. This is done for us not only so that people can obtain great rewards by it, but as evidence that we have been valiant in that most valiant of causes.

This can be done even in these latter days because the people can be taught and led by the Holy Ghost, who is the third member of the Godhead. It is my job to state the existence of the Holy Ghost and to state His purpose. It is my opinion that anyone who doesn't understand this, will, at the very least, be missing out on something important.

I realize that this notion might fly in the face of a self-confessed dreamer like John Lennon, who wrote lyrics like: "Imagine that there's no heaven. It isn't hard to do. Nothing to kill or die for and no religion too."

But so be it. John Lennon was a mortal man and I would say a very creative man, but he was not all-wise in a historical or a theological sense, and if I actually met Him in the next world and asked Him his thoughts on the matter now, I think that he would be the first to admit that now his perspectives would be the thoughts of a deeply religious man.

I will not judge the character of John Lennon, or most other artists, for speaking out or singing about an ideal world that they would like to live in, or even think about. But at the end of it all, when all the cards have been played, I think it will be seen by everyone that actual

WISDOM will rule the day. By that, I mean that true laws of God will rule over the only permanent realm that there is.

That permanent realm is also called the Eternal realm. To learn what is necessary to abide in that realm might take us a lifetime to learn. Nevertheless we will valiantly try to learn it while knowing we are in good company. We will have Jesus Christ at our side then, as well of all of the righteous saints who have ever lived. It would not be fair for a just God to command us to do things and not tell us about the supreme benefits that will be gained.

A secular person who lives a secular life and who dies, but is not connected with anything spiritual, does not have permanence and does not have large amounts of joy if they did not accept spiritual authority, but chose instead to be involved only with worldly authority.

That person might have only an occasional spiritual prompting or spiritual ambition, but I ask, will that be enough to motivate that person to progress upwards? I don't know, but in my particular case, I will be a witness to the judgments of God, and even try to plan my own life to be in harmony with those righteous judgments.

I say that if the principles that people embrace are <u>not</u> approved by the Great Creator who is all-wise, then such promptings and ambitions can never be given permanent or 'Eternal status' because they are basically worthless. Is everyone entitled to his or her opinion? Yes, they are, but that doesn't mean that their opinions are true or right.

God has definite purposes and does not waste time with worthless things. The God who created us human beings in the first place will determine the revelations and promptings and ambitions that human beings receive, and will observe to what degree those who receive those revelations follow through on them. His judgments are, and will be, based upon His 'laws'. Those laws are sensible, fair, righteous and everlasting.

This section of my book is like an opening statement. Later on I will talk about other relevant things like the importance of families and the nature of morality, but for now, the things I have said so far are a part of the larger premise that God's laws are true and we need to obey them individually in order to be able to enter in to the highest kingdom of Heaven, and as a family and a community in order to be blessed by His favor. I also think that the sensibilities of those laws that I speak of are backed up by most of the world's major religions.

"no unclean thing can dwell with God."
– 1ˢᵗ Nephi 10:21 (Book of Mormon)

Thus, it seems that God has very high standards. Would you, as a disciple, want it any other way?

C H A P T E R 2

Islands in the Stream

(COLLABORATORS WANTED)

Aldous Huxley once said, "No man is an island". On the other hand, it might be said that all men are islands. If that is true, it seems that the connections we make with other islands are of great importance, especially if those are the only connections that we have.

<u>Good</u> connections should be nurtured. Bad connections should be trashed as long as they remain bad. Good connections should be made with good islands (beings) who are humble and good and deserve respect, as opposed to making connections with selfish islands, those whose concerns are only with themselves. Likewise, there are also 'wild card islands' in life who may, or may not, be well meaning, but who are, in various ways, unstable or unpredictable.

'Wild cards' (wild humans) are usually unacquainted or unconcerned with the more noble aspects of living as human beings. That means that when we form relationships, they should be formed with people who are noble and respectable beings who are concerned with noble and 'creative' activities. Those relationships should be nourished everyday and our loyalty to those people must be occasionally displayed. Thus, it really is all about attitude, even a 'joint attitude'.

In order to be worthy of making good connections with good people, there is always some responsibility on our part. There is always a responsibility to use our thinking abilities and to have an accompanying 'intellectual passion' and even a mutual passion when we are working with other people on a joint project.

Our passion for this kind of clear thinking and a clear and good purpose should be evident in our words and our actions. Exercising this kind of purpose should be the top priority for all of us. It might also be called 'wisdom' as it applies to things that make use of our best skills. Even 'peculiar' wisdom like exercising a different kind of humor counts.

I worked for many years in a show band that travelled around the country. All four of us had different talents, but the ways that we were mostly appreciated by our audiences were the times when we combined those talents in simultaneous ways during our shows. As we did that we firmed a kind of bond with each other, not only professionally, but we developed friendships with each other as well.

Such bonds can be an important in the success of anything. Friendships are usually one of the main parts of our lives. It includes being on the same basic wavelength as certain other people. Our civilized and friendly efforts are capable of displacing the wild and untamed areas of our relationships and of the human imagination.

Reason, intelligent thinking, passion (including a love for humor), should always be prime considerations in matters of creativity. If you do not keep that in mind, then self-justification, pride and anger can eventually, and naturally become a big part of our PDM (Personality Default Mode).

Creative writing is the vehicle that I like to use most of the time. Also, there is never a cohesive textbook involved in creativity, so learning, including exercising discernment is necessary for progress. This is because a topic or a story can be a vague or a complicated thing. That is not always a bad thing because it can force the individual to figure things out clearly. Some people do that very well at that and some don't. Can I do it? I could do it at various stages of my life, but I do have my limitations and I am usually aware what those limitations are.

I was moderately successful in the world of entertainment /theatre some years ago, but I don't think I ever reached my potential. The chemistry I had with my fellow band members was good, but it was not good enough for an extraordinary breakthrough in the very competitive industry that was 'entertainment'. I count my blessings though when I realize that I got through it all relatively unscathed.

Entertaining and collaboration involves intellectual passion, humor and even a humble perspective. Whatever talent we have will eventually come to the fore when we are put under the pressure of having hundreds of people watching us, but still, the attitudes I spoke about are necessary for us to contemplate. These attitudes will come out in large part by our actions because words alone can only go so far.

Nevertheless, I find pleasure in working with words and doing so in a civilized way, as opposed to manipulating words in order to achieve some kind of hidden agenda. When I get good new ideas as I am writing, it is like climbing to a new spiritual 'plateau' and that is always a quite delight.

This is not only good for my peace of mind, but it can actually be a <u>necessary</u> thing for a man like me who wants to be free from being enveloped, or encompassed, by influences that are outside of my control. For example, people who are preoccupied with sex or drugs, or who are over-preoccupied with anything, are good examples of people who have a tendency to 'split their focus' in their writings and formulations. This not only produces inferior writing, but can also result in disasters in the performance area. That is assuming that the performers are not just on 'automatic pilot' and rely on repeating well established routines that were formulated a long time ago.

A writer or creator who uses a plethora of reference points is always in danger of splitting their focus. It can even mean that the writer might lose a large segment of their audience if they try to please everybody. Thus, I say that the best results will come with making connections with other collaborating 'islands' who have similar tastes and similar values. This is a serious matter for writers and artists who entertain people for a living. Failure in the entertainment realm never leaves an artist with a good feeling.

Some of the hardest working people I have ever met are comedians. That is because they are always trying to think of a new 'bit'. They might even fall into the trap of dedicating their whole life to it, body and soul. I am glad I never got into that to such an extreme.

Does dedication and hard work overcome all difficulties? I would have to say no. There are ways you may be able to exhibit your higher and/or your most comedic self, but most people cannot do that on public on a consistent basis and so they often just give up and try a new profession, and that might be okay. Or they might end up doing menial jobs while still looking for that 'big break' in their old age. The same may be true for anyone who chooses to go into any kind of 'high risk' business.

Distractions are always a handicap for any man or woman and it doesn't matter what kind of work they are involved in. The man named Nephi in the Book of Mormon was a great man. Even he admitted that he had carnal urges that are not healthy. He experienced connections with many 'undesirable islands'. Some of those islands were described as evil and he used the word 'encompassed' to describe how they influenced him.

> *"I am encompassed about, because of the temptations and the sins which do so easily beset me."*
>
> *– 2 Nephi 4:18*

'Encompassed' is a powerful word. The word could mean 'totally enveloped'. Is it possible that this 'encompassing process' could become something that we will need to deal with in our own lives as creator of anything, whether that creation is literary, or romantic or in a business sense or in a sense of anything?

I have no doubt of that. To be <u>unable</u> to work cohesively and effectively with other people is a weakness, but it is not uncommon and so that is not always easy to overcome. That is because are not always mature adults, even thought they are adults. In ways, some of us are still little children when it comes down to the basic frustrations that life presents us with. We are still young islands in the stream and the wise islands, who could positively influence us, are often content to live in isolation.

When I see signs of being encompassed by another island, I try to recall, or reestablish, my mission statement. In brief, a mission statement of mine might be to try to implement your 'love and passion for knowledge' with your desire to live a life that has respectful relationships with other islands, either co-workers or audiences.

That passion for respect and the sharing of values needs to bear sway immediately in your thoughts and in your personality. Hopefully, those things will mesh with the thoughts and values of other islands. If that doesn't happen with me, as a collaborator, I will be nothing but a 'failed collaborator'. That has happened to me, but I try not to take it too personally because having good chemistry with a talented collaborator is often not easy to find.

I do <u>not</u> believe however that show business or giving constant performances of any kind are the main purpose that people should have in their lives. I believe that to write something that shows talent or cleverness is a good thing, but mainly, people should be more concerned with actually living a good or righteous life. That is what will count the most when the final score is tallied. This is mainly so we can sleep well at night and sleep with a clear conscience.

I like to tell stories sometimes about the years that I spent in the entertainment business as well as my years teaching music in schools. Now that I am a minister in my church though, that is where I most enjoy focusing my attention. Being a minister and being an entertainer, and even being a teacher, have many similarities for me. All three people are all the center of attention in their own realms. That seems odd because I was rather withdrawn as a youth and never expressed any desire to be the center of attention.

Well, here I am. Hey, look at me!

I guess everybody likes to laugh. Everybody likes to be intrigued. Everybody likes to have his or her heart touched. As far as my professions go, it is that third 'like' was the one that I found the most rewarding. I am referring to, 'what touches people's hearts'. When that happens, that is when I feel I am actually making a difference in people's lives.

That is the main key to living a happy and fulfilling life. It has been said that: 'It is better to 'act' than be acted upon.' Good ideas, even divinely inspired ideas, can excite another person, but are those ideas and the person who they come from, 'consistent' with a person's general nature and personal faith? They do, in fact need to be consistent with people's spirituality or things will just not work.

Thus, having similar contexts with other islands in the stream are essential for finding, or creating, good relationships and good overall products.

Then there are the distractions that I mentioned; mainly the distractions that have the power to encompass a person. If I am aware, I will know when those 'encompassing' ones begin to appear. Thus, it is possible for me resist them and begin to write good things down, even creative things to counteract those unholy things.

It works for me, but I know I must use the proper tools of my imagination. I am talking about things like measuring tools for example, even the tools that measure the differences between right and wrong. Measuring differences between various moral factors is what a 'spiritual craftsperson' would do, as opposed to employing the simple tools of force like a hammer and nails, tools that a simple laborer would use.

That laborer might be a hard working laborer, but he or she also needs to be a craftsperson. Once the craftsperson <u>measures</u> his or her boundaries carefully, then he or she acts and puts the tools of the trade to work, whether it is a hammer and nails, or a saw, or whatever. He, or she, then goes from <u>thinking to</u> <u>doing</u>.

We need 'hammer and nails people' in life, but even more so we need writers, technicians, mathematicians, engineers, and even people who think clearly through all of the aspects of complicated issues that we encounter in life. I am talking about skilled tradespeople here, but I am also talking about working with PEOPLE OF CHARACTER. I am talking here about mentors, friends and thinking people who understand the moral complexities in life and who know the difference between right and wrong.

When we have good moral connections that gives us the opportunity to connect with even people who are probably higher connections. If we want to learn good things and reason with skill, why not begin with studying a person who was the ultimate in goodness and the ultimate in reasoning?

Yes, Jesus was a carpenter, but he also had twelve collaborators at His side, and many more too. He was a simple tradesman, but He also had another distinction. He was the savior and redeemer of the world. The job that he did if establishing His church on the Earth was truly, as the author James E. Talmage called it, 'a marvelous work and a wonder'.

Some people might say that as I am a minister my opinion is biased on this matter, but so be it. In any case you can check out His philosophy any time you like and see if it is lacking in any way. It is very important though to search through a 'reliable source' that has sensible answers to life's questions from the very beginning up until the very end.

As far as man not being an island goes, that may be so, but I think that sometimes it is okay to be an island as long as we feel the love of God in us. In that case, we will never really be alone, even in a fast flowing stream.

So I say that it can be okay to be an island, but it is even better to be a well-connected island. I don't know if making certain connections will solve our problems or not, but I do know that some connections are better than other connections. Also, the connections that are a part of the vast network that contains true religious doctrine those are the best kind of connections to have.

CHAPTER 3

The Good Life and Preparing For It

SUBTITLES:
- My Stated Goal
- Receiving proper instructions;
- Maintenance strategies
- Becoming motivated day by day
- Rules
- Warnings

"Therefore be perfect even as your Father".
– Matthew 5: 48

Perhaps there is some kind of strategy that can make perfection come easier. To begin with, I have three suggestions.

1. Set a goal, a righteous goal.
2. Seek to receive proper instructions and then obey those instructions.
3. Investigate maintenance strategies, which includes dealing with memories.

There is however, something that is outside of ourselves in this equation. I am talking here about the grace of God. Perfection comes by His grace. Assuming you have the humility and the knowledge to make that connection, let us go back to the other three principles.

My Stated Goal

Like everyone, I desire to be happy, but specifically there are certain methods that I employ to increase my odds of achieving success in the matter. I do this by making a connection with my higher power every day.

There are many ways we can seek the guidance we need from God. Initially, we first need to ask for His help. Say something definitive like – "I will seek the Spirit of the Lord." That is stating your intention and is also a way of asking your Heavenly Father if He approves of your desire. It's a start. After we state our good intention, we then ask God to send us inspiration or counsel and even the good spiritual feelings that go along with His considerations. Those will appear in some kind of spiritual form, which is, naturally, invisible.

This is a good way to get God's attention and perhaps actually feel His presence, maybe not at first, but eventually good things will start to happen. God's grace will be there if we are humble beforehand and grateful afterwards.

Sometimes, when I arise in the morning, I, personally, often recite the first two commandments in the Bible and often the first person present as in - "I will love the Lord my God with all my heart, might, mind and strength, and I will love my neighbor as myself". That can set the tone for my day subconsciously, if not consciously. I don't really need to contemplate this verse too hard. I can just recite it and let it sink in, and it will make a difference in my day. Thus, it becomes a matter of making a connecting to an actual power that is higher than us.

A person can state their short-term goals along with their long term goals. If a person's main goal is a romantic one that may be fine, depending how clear you are in the issues, but if you mix you're your romantic goals with your career-based goals, that might give a double focus to the answer. It will be your choice in any case how to phrase a question. Take your time and carefully think about what your first focus should be. If you are unsure of your question, then the Lord will be unsure too and may not give you an answer until you get things straight in your own mind.

Receiving Proper Instruction

If I should ask a random person if there is any such thing as receiving proper instruction in life, many of those people would say 'No'. At the same time many of those people would probably say 'Yes'. The question therefore is probably then a moot question – unanswerable.

You may want to have a specific response, but that is really your own business and God never wants to meddle in someone else's affairs, especially if their future depends upon the answer.

Thus, I say, give Him a break. Figure out exactly what you want an then ask Him if He would advise you on the best way to get it. If He doesn't answer you then that is your answer. In other words, it is up to you. He cannot make up your mind and He cannot make up the mind of the object of your affection.

But is it a moot or unanswerable question? That can depend upon the accuracy and good sense and the spiritual affirmation if whatever in-formation has been given to you. Thus, it will be up to the individual to carefully study that information from all angles and do not let yourself be convinced of the truth of that information until you are actually <u>convinced</u> of it, while at the same time being open minded enough to study other appealing church doctrines and compare the schools of thought.

To an individual investigator I would say, go to a church, a good and sound church. Be sure, as much as you can, that it is a church that you feel you can trust because there is a good and gentle spirit that pervades the building. Ask questions. Think spiritually and ask God in your mind if the church is one that is based upon the spirit of Truth. You may not get an answer at first, but if you keep on asking, there is probably going to be some kind of sign that is given to you. It might not be a strong sign, but it will probably be a sign that feels good in your heart. If a strong answer does not come to you, ask more questions and don't give up the search. Also, I recommend that you feel free to rationally compare the doctrine of various churches at any time and seek revelations from the Spirit on doctrinal matters. Seek those answers on a spiritual level and not strictly on an intellectual level.

Study the gospel in private and/or with others. Pray often and seek for personal revelation. For the sake of your own clarity, keep a journal and write down your best thoughts. Study the issues so you will be prepared to discuss those issues intelligently. Learn from good teachers and mentors. It is more important that those teachers and mentors are able to touch your heart than to touch your intellect or your ego.

Maintenance Strategies

This is a piece about 'mentorship'. A friend of mine died recently and I found myself in a state of grief. This was unusual for me because normally I am the kind of guy who does not believe in being upset by things that are definitely out of my control. This situation was a little different.

My friends name was Dave and we met because he was a fellow musician and we made a lot if music together over the years. I have known many professional musicians over the years and I can say that I actually enjoyed the company of the vast majority of them. I will also say that there were only a few of the musicians I knew that I actually admired on a personal level as well as a professional level. Dave was such a person.

He was an excellent musician who played accordion on a world class level. He also owned a recording studio in Winnipeg, where I lived, and where I recorded much of my music. He engineered the productions and assisted me with overdubs on his accordion. Most importantly, Dave was also was a fine human being in my opinion. He had a flashy smile and a healthy laugh and he never said anything bad about other people as far as I knew. He was financially successful too. He had a nice house, a good wife and a beautiful garden where he spent many hours working on the land.

Perhaps it was because he came from parents who were immigrants from the Ukraine that Dave was a conservative thinker. He had no use for the totalitarian communism that ruled over Russia and the Ukraine over the last century. He understood that government control would eventually bring about tyranny in a country one hundred per cent of the time.

Dave never preached his political beliefs to the masses, but he was not afraid to state them when the occasion called for it. Thus, he was a mentor for me in many ways, as a musician, as a businessman, as a fun loving guy who was enthusiastic about his heritage and loved the freedom that his family found when they moved to Canada.

Because of the great respect I had for him, I regarded Dave as both a mentor and a friend. After he passed away, I wished that I had spent more time socializing with him and his wife, but he lived across town and we did not socialize as much as I would have wanted to. It often seems that we are prevented from enjoying the company of people who we admire because of our business commitments.

In short, I just wanted to say to young people that they should seek out relationships with hard working people of conviction and join them in their efforts to preserve and exercise their feelings of independence and individual initiative. The companionship of such people who find joy in doing good things, and smile when they do those things, brings out the best in all of us.

The point I am making here is that people who we really admire are the people who wet our standards of value. If you don't have anyone who you truly value, you should keep you eyes open for people like that and hold on to them once you find them. Don't worry about them rejecting you because if you do really admire them, then they would not do that. It is not, or should not be a part of their character. Instead, they will be your calm in a storm.

Becoming Motivated (Day By Day)

On becoming motivated: Here is a morning tip to start you off. When you go to bed at night think about a project you would like to work on the next day. Write in your journal an entry where you may list a few of the details of what you intend to think about regarding your project.

As you wake up in the morning, let a few of those ideas blossom in your mind and see if there are any ideas or details that might come into your mind that will advance those good thoughts. This act alone should make you excited. Hold that thought. Feel it in your body and let the excitement of it cause your body in bed to feel anticipation. Give your body a stretch to let it know that a starter bell has sounded in your mind. Get up and start writing in more detail.

Rules

Here is more food for thought about a previous essay about how we can receive proper instructions in life. Allow me to ask you a personal question. What drives you? What inspires you? What motivates you to get up in the morning and go to a job that may be compromising, at best, and involves hard work that allows you little time to do the things that you really want to do? Say that you do actually find a creative job that you like. If you do that then ask yourself 'what moves you?' 'What propels you?' Take time to think about it if you need to.

I will not be able to hear your answer because I am on the other side of this book in a mutual time/space warp (sometimes an inconvenient situation), but you do not need my approval. I assume that you have some sensible and valuable motivating forces behind all of the things that you do.

To some people this question of motivation does not really matter. They are quite content with who they are and how their lives are going and they need no outsider to cast doubts on their personal state of well being. and I say that I sincerely congratulate them on their satisfied state and I wish them well.

But looking at the rates of suicide, divorce, violence, crime, single parent families, abortions, international tensions, and general unhappiness in the world, I think that there are many people who have need to ask themselves this question on a regular basis so that they might monitor all situations and try to remedy those ones in which they find their personal happiness quotient lacking. We all need to ask ourselves from time to time if we are on the right track or if we could use some kind of well thought out corrections in our thoughts or in our attitudes.

Personally, I try to live by righteous principles and I believe that those principles are actually heaven sent and revealed to us by prophets and some very wise men and women. I am not without my own flaws and lazy tendencies, but nevertheless, I do believe that it would be ideal if all of us tried to live by as much righteousness as we can. What a wonderful world that would be.

Warnings

I like to discuss revelations in my writings and speculate in when and how they can happen and to whom and how they work. Revelations, as I understand the word, means that human beings who are worthy of it, may actually receive revealed truth from our creator who is our God. These revealed truths are, most of the time quite beautiful to experienced and will always contain, in one form or another, the wisdom of the heavens.

Not all revelations however can be pleasant all of the time. Sometimes they will come as warnings, depending upon who the receiver of the warning and their situation. I will give you one example if a warning revelation that I had in the middle if the night very recently.

As I have said elsewhere in this book, revelations can come in the form of warnings. These revelations can sometimes be frightening and hence, not seen as positive messages, but negative ones. There is no need to worry. This kind of message is probably there for a good reason. It might even be there to help you to realize the gravity of the situation in your life. Most lives, if not all, do have some gravity in them. The revelation might even be there to cause you to 'WAKE UP'.

I will give you one example of a 'warning revelation' that I received very recently. I went in to see my family doctor about a skin lesion that I had on my face. I was afraid that it might be skin cancer. The doctor did a biopsy and things went, pretty much, according to plan. While I was there I told him about having a sharp pain in my side when I moved around too much. The doctor said immediately that he was going to prescribe for me a 'muscle relaxant' to help me cope with that. It was called 'Baclofen'.

I took the pills for about three days, but there was not a lot of improvement in my side pain. On the fourth day however, I had a nightmare in the middle of the night. I often have dreams where I feel that I am in the presence of a higher force, or even a Divine Being on rare occasions. It is always a very positive feeling. Those are usually very good experiences and I felt that something good was about to happen as I lay on my bed in a state of semi-consciousness. 'Something good' did not happen though, quite the opposite in fact.

I began to have a good feeling of communion with the higher power that I just spoke about, but then something went wrong. It was like my brain was starting to malfunction and the communication that I normally felt in that mental state had been 'cut-off'. There was nothing there anymore. I felt that my 'personal identity', or the 'core of my being' had DIED. Only a person who was actually involved in something like that and knew a few things about it could understand it.

I was not able to direct my thoughts the way I wanted to at that moment. It was very unusual for me and it was also very frightening. The thought even entered my mind that I might be dying. I woke up shortly thereafter, but I was still very shaken and alarmed about what had just happened. I still acknowledged that my death might be immanent, so I thought I had better clean up some of my affairs just in case.

A few days later, I went to see another doctor about an unrelated matter. He had requested a list of any new medications that I might be on. I showed him the bottle of Baclofen that my family doctor had given me. He knew right away what they were.

I told him about my nightmare. He recommended that I get off those pills because they have been known to cause problems in the mental processes of certain patients. I immediately agreed with him and thanked him for his advice.

In previous hospital stays, I had always refused any anti-depressant pills that doctors prescribed. I didn't trust them and I didn't believe that doctors had the right to play around with people's brains. I am a religious man and I have my reasons for that. I also believed that, in the beginning, God gave human beings a pure spirit that was in His likeness, but in a much more basic form. That 'clean spirit' was necessary for a one on one communication with Divinity. For me, at that time, that 'clean Spirit' was not there anymore and I was worried, not only for my mortal life, but for my spiritual life.

I had heard in the past that the religion of Scientology was adamant about their church members not partaking of anti-depression drugs that tampered with the brain, and I was, at that point fully understanding of why. I even wondered if, maybe, doctors, so as to take away any fears that people had, were now calling those 'brain drugs' 'muscle relaxants'.

That would be a more acceptable term, but the potential damage was still there. I lost some respect for the medical profession on that day, but I did gain some respect for the Church of Scientology that they would go against the social grain and talk to people about medical mishaps. In any case, I went out of that office that day feeling much better and I had a lot more hope for the future. So what was the message I received by that dream? I figured it was something like – SOMETHING IS PLAYING WITH YOUR PRECIOUS MIND. DON'T LET IT DO THAT.

CHAPTER 4

A Simple Plan

SUBTITLES:
- ➲ Two Simple Steps
- ➲ Anxiety Dreams and Navel Gazing

HERE ARE <u>TWO SIMPLE STEPS</u> TO GAIN A HEALTHY PERSPECTIVE ON DAILY LIFE)

1. Come to an understanding of good spiritual principles that will help you personally, and then contemplate those principles to the exclusion of all else. Let 'all else' come into the picture only when it is necessary. Let the higher thoughts linger in your mind for as long as possible. Let them simmer there in their own time and you can expand on them as you write in your journal.

2. Know that your understanding of a good and wise principle could be all that you need <u>today</u>. If you find it, you can meditate on it, but here is no need to search for something more. Find someone who can appreciate that principle and tell them about it. Explain it in the most succinct way that you can.

Every night I go through a period of deep sleep. I guess everyone does to some degree, but for me, because I am prone to experiencing all kinds of night dreams. That seems to be something that I need to reckon with. On some occasions, that dream space in my mind can be like a dark wasteland or a desert, but at other times, I do have a light that shines in my mind that will allow me to see things, both beautiful and ugly things as they apply to my circumstances at that particular time. If I ever have a nightmare or see an ugly image like a wasteland, I try to summon my light and let it shine on the wasteland and watch it evolve into something shiny and delightful.

My dreams have always been vivid. Things sometimes happen in my dreams that are out of my control. My dream state can be deep. On occasion, I can even lose my sense of identity and another realm can come upon me.

One thing I need to do is to control my thought patterns. If I have a nasty dream image that I cannot seem to get away from, I must learn to 'shelve it'. I might just get up and think about something else or even read something.

In any case, I say that if I am going to activate my mind even as I am in my sleeping hours, I try to let my thinking be concerned with something meaningful and not just incoherent or irrelevant images like I find in some night dreams.

In some dreams that I have, the situations I find myself in do not have a good resolution. I call them 'anxiety dreams'. I would even compare some of those dream situations to 'the valley of the shadow of death' in Psalms 23. It is a frightening place.

My point is that the world is a dangerous place and that danger can come from outside of ourselves or from inside of ourselves. I would not recommend that anyone willingly go onto a realm where danger is everywhere, no matter how brave you might think you are.

Let us look at the tiny common spider, who cannot harm other creatures by attacking them, but who can spin a web that can entangle other creatures hold them in bondage until it decides that it is time for them to be devoured.

At the same time, I say, do not let your <u>fear</u> of spiders or other menacing creatures keep you in a mental bondage, one where you feel helpless and destined to become a permanent victim of some kind. Don't let anything from the known world or from the unknown world 'bully your mind'. Your mind and your ability to control your mind, are the greatest tools you will need to gain freedom in this life.

It is only a few simple good thoughts that you will need to establish jurisdiction over what you let into your mind. If you expand on those thoughts, it will become more than a simple thought. It will become a simple plan, and it will provide you with many hours of 'clean' meditation.

My night dreams seem to present me with some odd situations sometimes, even ridiculous ones. Perhaps I was designated (or condemned) in the pre-existence, to walk through those places occasionally. The best way to escape from a bad place is a thing I call 'substitution'. You are a free-thinking individual and you always have a choice between thinking about something naughty or useless, or else thinking about something pleasant and productive.

You will also need to repent of any past action that might stimulate a bad memory or a bad dream experience that would enter into your mind. A bad memory is like a <u>fire</u>. It captures your attention. It spreads because it has momentum when it burns.

Momentum is a weird thing. The human eye always follows anything that has momentum. It can even be somewhat hypnotic. Thus, I say that ignoring certain things even though they may be moving is all right. A fire needs oxygen to keep burning. <u>A common form of 'spiritual oxygen' is your attention</u>. Don't give wicked thoughts or idle thoughts your attention. What will happen when you cut off a fire's oxygen supply? It will extinguish itself. I am talking here about things that attract us. Action or momentum always attracts our attention.

On the other hand some images serve us only in their ability to 'distract us'.

I remember when my baby brother was about two years old, He loved to watch television. A lot. If he was watching something that made him curious, he would continue to watch that program until it was over. If I picked him up and held him so that he was facing another direction, and not one where the television was in his line of vision, he would twist his body around until he was positioned himself in a place where he could actually see the program he had been watching before. Was he addicted to watching television? I don't know, but I know that when he grew up he got a job where he worked as a movie/ television reviewer for a local newspaper. True story.

How many of us are held by an image of some kind that attracts us or makes us curious? I think that there are probably many of us whose minds work like that. I also would wager that the devil knows this about human beings and he would try to accommodate us in this particular pastime or habit whenever he could. At the same time he would, through media corporations, control the content that was shown on that television or on a movie screen.

There are various kinds of momentum. How about social media? Is that action? Does that little screen in someone's hand have momentum? It absolutely does. The key is that it is mental momentum. The mind is being attacked by a barrage of images and ideas, many of them half-baked and some coming from left field. Can a young impressionable person ignore such things? Some can and some cannot. There are statistics that show that the rate if teenage suicide has risen sharply since the invention of the 'smart phone' in the year 2008. It has risen anywhere from 50% to 300%. This is a serious social problem that can often have tragic results.

My point in this essay is that we should not let ourselves be overly influenced by things that are going on 'outside of ourselves', especially those things that have momentum, or 'flash', or charm, or even humor. On the other hand, it is a very wise thing to accept good counsel from someone who is trustworthy, especially if you are lucky enough to know someone who is 'good' enough to give that counsel.

A dream can be like the flow of a river and my mind is like a vessel that is floating on that river. Even if I desire to be free from my journey, my will is not enough to stop the flow of the river, so then I will need to get off the boat and embrace the dry land. But is it a bad thing to become a 'land lubber?

For a natural born sailor, that might be difficult to resist, but would it be dangerous? I don't know, but personally, I just don't like the notion of being held captive in some audio/visual realm that originated from somewhere outside of myself. When I recognize that I am a responding to something that did not originate with me, I might need to ask myself, 'Who is in control here? If I am not really in control here, then 'who is?'

I have become more aware of this mental wasteland in recent years. I suspect it might have been there in my youth to a lesser degree, but I just ignored it because I did not really understand what was going on at the time. This was mostly because I was not experienced enough to figure it all out.

In my later years, I accepted the gospel of Jesus Christ, which gave my life meaning and basically, made me a wiser person in many ways and helped me to become better acquainted with reality. Did that awareness stop any evil penetrations from entering into my mind? I would say, partly, but not totally. The devil knows us and he knows me and he knows where the vulnerable parts of my mind are. I have no doubt about that. Although the devil is wicked, he is still cunning, and he chooses innocent victims mostly because of their innocence or their gullibility.

When young people become aware of the devastating consequences that innocence can have, it is often too late to do anything about it. There are only two things that can prevent such willful destruction. Those are 1. Having the self - restraint to <u>not</u> get involved with any sensual, or wicked, ideas and 2. accepting the great gift of repentance which comes from above and thus, creating a clean slate for yourself.

I once heard Dennis Prager say, '<u>there is power in boredom</u>'. I don't think that he meant that boredom is a 'good' power. We might think that boredom is only a natural thing. Well, maybe it is, but is a natural thing a good thing? The scriptures say, "the natural man is an enemy to God". (Mosiah 3:19)

That seems to be one of the principles in life that consistently shows up in our minds as we travel on our journey. Hopefully though, we will have the ability to recognize it when it does show up. We always need to see the higher perspectives. The lower perspective is destructive, but only when we refuse to resist it. This applies not only to carnal thoughts, but also to depressing thoughts, mundane thoughts, and feelings of hopelessness.

If we do not have the proper tools to overcome that state of anxiety or boredom or feelings of inadequacy, then that state will become an enemy, and we will then need to seek allies to overcome that enemy. In some cases, the allies we choose will have their appeal, but some of them could, in reality, turn out to be <u>allies to our enemies</u> instead of allies to us.

I give one example that fits this description. It <u>is alcohol</u>. You can think of other enemies I am sure, but most of them, like alcohol, or drugs, are centered on certain pleasurable activities that take advantage of the weakness of human pride and the appeal of false stimulations or false expectations.

It may be natural for people to seek excitement. We often begin that search by activating our imaginations. We can fantasize about many things, but that doesn't take any real talent or organizational skills. Truly enjoyable activities though must be sensible activities that will require organization and the setting of priorities, and an appreciation of the simple things in life.

If we don't have good organizational skills, then someone, or something else, will present some different skills to us. There will usually be lots of people applying for that job. Few of those people, or spirits, will have good resumes for the job.

The problem there is that unless your imagination has been blessed by a wise and powerful and loving being, it will be of no good use to you. It can even be a curse to you, no matter how much you may have chosen to value it at some time in the past.

That may have been a time from your past life when you had basic control over things, but over time our innocence will usually fade and a brand new game begins, even one that you were not expecting.

Anxiety DreamsaAnd Navel Gazing

After I wrote my second book I began thinking more about the spiritual influences in my life, good ones as well as bad ones. In my mind I expanded on some of the good principles I discovered. Thus, I wrote out a simple plan for anyone who suffers from anxiety dreams or boredom and would like to extricate themselves from hostile environments or fantasy environments or meaningless navel gazing during their resting or contemplative hours.

If you find it necessary to contemplate the same good principal the same principle on successive days – so be it. There is nothing wrong with that, as long as you are not just being redundant and boring yourself.

If you are boring yourself, stop doing it. There are thousand if other good adventures and interesting people in life that you can focus your attention on.

Good principles and guidelines should be occasionally revisited in our minds though whenever we feel the need for some kind of 'positive spiritual or mental refreshment'. There are hundreds of things that we could choose to contemplate, even enough to last the rest if your life and beyond that. Thus, we should treat our good past experiences like old friends who come into our minds for a short visit.

There is one quote from the New Testament and it is from the angels who were present at the birth of Jesus Christ in Bethlehem.

> *"Fear not: for, behold, I bring you tidings of great joy, which shall be to all people." "And suddenly there was with the angel a multitude of the heavenly host praising God and saying, Glory to God in the Highest, and on Earth peace, goodwill toward men".*
>
> *– Luke 2: 10 – 14*

This last line was not something irrelevant. It was the literal reason why Jesus came to earth. It was to bring glory to God, peace and goodwill toward men. Why is this quote not heard or analyzed very much? Would you not think that it deserves much discussion? A good discussion that would include some remedial suggestions would seem extremely important. It seems to me that would be much more beneficial that repeating vague buzz words like 'love' and 'tolerance'. This is one example of a topic for a relevant and stimulating discussion.

Courage brother. Courage sister. Your 'resistance connection' can always become activated and then you can be free from getting into a rut and you can be free to discuss 'things that matter'. Resist the urge to 'sit on your duff'. SPEAK UP. You may find however, that you are not as resistant as you used to be. Take heart. It can be done. Let us begin by making a list of topics.

Things to contemplate:

1. Firstly, contemplate you area part of the Spirit of God. Do this in conjunction with contemplating your own personal spirit. That is what you know about your spirit and what you still need to know. Use examples from the scriptures to help you. Also use the words of wisdom that are given to you by prophets from old times and from the present day. If you should need a real 'kick in the pants, contemplate the amazing life of Jesus Christ and ruminate on the tremendous sacrifice that He made for you.

Thirty one more things you may choose to contemplate –

2. Contemplate your personal blessings.
3. Contemplate the two most important things in life - joy and permanence. Joy is your responsibility. Permanence is God's gift for you. Be grateful for that gift.
4. Contemplate how you can help, serve and encourage other people.
5. Contemplate bliss lines and strength lines on an emotional level (as they are explained in my book 'Life Goes On'.)
6. Contemplate the pyramid and upward spiral of life and how you can use that progression in the most positive ways.
7. Contemplate the snakes and ladders of life and how you can make use of the ladders and, at the same time, avoid the snakes.
8. Contemplate the gift of the gospel and the establishment of the true church and the sacrifices that were made to bring the true church into being.
9. Contemplate the beauty of nature.

10. Contemplate your inevitable death and your permanent resting place. That resting place will be one of peace if you have followed the right path. That path is also a gift that has been blessed for your sake.

11. Contemplate principles of meaning and principles of non-meaning and make a list of those examples.

12. Contemplate the glorious place called heaven and what that might consist of. Also contemplate the 'high' things in life. You may contemplate the low things too, but do that only to keep you humble as you come to realize how small you are in the grand scheme of things.

13. Contemplate your family (if appropriate), and the true friends that you have. Also contemplate your 'spiritual team' If you have one. If you don't have one, try to seek one out.

14. Contemplate Gods and Goddesses and those who are worthy of such titles (or have been sanctified as such.)

15. Contemplate freedom and your role in preserving it in the world and what you might need to sacrifice in order to attain it.

16. Contemplate how to be strong and how you might show love and patience when dealing with people, learned or unlearned.

17. Contemplate the Holy temple, which is the blessed dwelling place of the Lord.

18. Contemplate your own gained knowledge and things you have learned that are of a certainty, and also how you managed to learn and maintain those things.

19. Contemplate how you have personally advanced over time.

20. Contemplate your body as a temple. Some people don't like their bodies or even resent them. When they abuse their bodies, they might be punishing them in a way.

21. Contemplate your unique mind and your humble personality.

22. Contemplate the knowledge that you have of your ancestors and of your heritage.

23. Contemplate the accomplishments and sacrifices of certain other characters whom you have read about or heard about, and who you identify with.
24. Contemplate your business and how you can use it to better serve yourself and others.
25. Contemplate your noblest passions and think of a time when you showed them.
26. Contemplate the gift of forgiveness.
27. Contemplate the gift of repentance.
28. Contemplate healing and pray for it, both for yourself and for others.
29. Contemplate the beauty of action, compassion, and joy.
30. Contemplate words and images that make you laugh.
31. Contemplate people you know who make you feel good.
32. Think of a time when you actually resisted something that was not good for you. Take a moment to congratulate yourself on that.

These are some of my own suggestions. You can always take more suggestions from other people.

These topics are there for purposes of your edification. If people don't make time for contemplating those things, they should. These principles are not about me being autocratic. I think they are important for everyone. Those principles are a pleasure to contemplate and it is only common sense to do so. It is certainly much more edifying to pursue a plan that stabilizes you and those around you rather than spending time on things that can only discourage you in the end.

In any case, I say please take time for such things. It will make you feel good when you do and you can feel even better when you ask the Lord to bless you and bless your thoughts on those matters and ask him to remind you of other things that He has blessed you with that you may have temporarily forgotten about.

God is very good at reminding people of important events, especially for those who have 'ears to hear' and a 'mind to remember'. If you are having dark feelings or feel like you might be being tormented, reading this essay might be just what you need.

C H A P T E R 5

The World of Spirits

The title of my book is 'What is my Purpose in Life'. To study this question, we must first look at what life actually consists of. There are elements in life that are physical elements or visible elements and there are elements that are unseen. When I write about 'entities' in life I am writing about 'living entities', seen or unseen. Living 'entities' can be seen and physically perceived or they can be invisible and exist only in spirit form. IE: Emotions like love and unity are not visible, but they are there.

Spirit beings are real beings in their own realms. That means that they can have cognition and in some cases actually influence ordinary people who do not have a secure foundation by projecting images onto their minds or their imaginations. Those spirits can influence people by the ideas or images that they project onto the imaginations of people, even reasonably normal people. Those images and influences can either be good or bad, but it is an attractive playground for bad, or troublemaking spirits who want to have an influence in the normal working world.

If a person does not recognize an invisible entity, or spirit, as being influential in reality, then that entity will have no immediate influence over a person who they are trying to influence.

That is because spirits don't have bodies. A spirit can only be an influence if it is 'allowed' to penetrate the mental realm of another entity or a host entity. This power of 'allowing' is some thing that must be addressed because it can determine exactly what entities we will choose to acknowledge in our minds. It could then possibly set the direction of where our freedom of choice will take us.

These image projections apply to feelings, emotions, ideas, attitudes and any other thing that a spirit wants us to recognize as legitimate. If that influence is good or benevolent then that goodness should be embraced, assuming it can display or give proof of those good and positive qualities over the long term. Spirits can have cognition and if it projects harmful thoughts then that spirit should be shunned or cast out or ignored by the host entity. That is probably the number one consideration for all vulnerable or curious people to be wary about.

A loving parent will attempt to protect and nurture their offspring in every way and hopefully the offspring will be thankful for that kindness, but we must be aware that every entity has its freedom to choose. He or she can choose a good way or a bad way, a right way or a wrong way, a constructive way or a destructive way. Sound simple? It is, but it can become complicated when we think about it for too long or go against the desires of our heavenly parents and the desires of the One who they have sent to us to be our redeemer.

Every one of us who is living on this earth will need to make decisions regarding our moral choices. The most important thing we can do in this regard is to develop a testimony of what is true and what is not true and if our heavenly progenitors really do care about us. We should then base our beliefs on that alone. That decision will be of an eternal consequence so it will require the strict attention of all who have agreed to participate in the plan of happiness and have chosen to come to earth and take on a physical body. That means you and me. Discovering your testimony might take a lot of time, but it cannot be ignored or it is entirely possible that spiritual problems and confusion will ensue.

Once we get to a certain state of awareness where we basically understand how we should act or react to the many kinds of stimuli that we are, or will be, presented with in our lives on a physical, mental, or emotional level, what is the next step? I say that it is to <u>recognize</u> all of those thoughts and beliefs that dwell in our conscious mind, our unconscious mind, and even on a higher, more spiritual level where we are able to let our conscious moral judgments have an influence on all if the things that we think and do. Thus, those firm beliefs actually become a part of us.

The only danger there is that we must not allow ourselves to think we know everything there is to know. We make a serious mistake when we do that because life is a constant learning experience for everybody and mistakes usually have vonsequences.

There is one main problem here. That is that if evil spirits were easy to see, we would avoid them or even fight them, but it happens that some spirits specialize in both deception and in hiding.

The most powerful being in the spirit world is the Holy Spirit, sometimes called the Holy Ghost. He is a good Spirit who is able and willing to give righteous counsel and promptings to all mortals who sincerely ask for it. Unfortunately, most human beings do not ask for it because they don't believe in His authority or else they don't even know who He is or don't know if He even exists.

If someone asks for a spirit to give them counsel, they will be playing with fire if they do not understand anything about the divine qualities that the Holy Ghost possesses. It takes many hours, and even many years to come to learn those things. On any case, the Holy Ghost is so powerful that He has been named the third part of the Godhead, which also includes the Father and the Son.

The Father stridently wants to protect the Holy Ghost. Thus, there is a verse in Mathew in the Bible that reads:

"Wherefore I say unto you, All manner of sin and blasphemy shall be forgiven unto men: but the blasphemy against the Holy Ghost shall not be forgiven unto men. And whosoever speaketh a word against the Son of man, it shall be forgiven him: but whosoever speaketh against the Holy Ghost, it shall not be forgiven him, neither in this world, neither in the world to come.

- Matthew 12: 31,32

Thus, we must take heed because our Father is extremely protective of the Holy Ghost. While this admonition does not include the 'ignoring' of the Holy Ghost, I would submit to you that that is what many people do, and I would personally list that as a serious issue.

Some knowledge of the spirit world however, can be granted to us by the study of the Divine Nature and in coming to an understanding of the Godhead. This knowledge has been given to us in a certain scripture.

"The Father and the Son have bodies of flesh and bones. The Holy Ghost does not have a physical body and that allows him to dwell within us."

– Doctrine and Covenants 130: 22

Now, if you want to look it up, you can do so. I am not being presumptuous here. I just cannot think of any other way that the Godhead could work.

When we speak to the Lord in prayer we know that He is on a higher plane than we are, and so He will speak to us only through the Spirit of the Holy Ghost. He might even be called the Lord's Chief Communications Officer.

As a prelude to this essay, I would also like to give a warning to all readers not to take any information on this subject lightly. That is because not all spirits who inhabit, the Spirit world are good spirits.

Some of them are mischievous and some could even be called evil. Evil spirits follow the devil.

The devil, or Lucifer, has been called 'the father of all lies' and there are many evil and deceptive things going on in his realm. I will not list any examples of that because the scope of evil spirits is extremely large and their strategies are devious and subtle and too numerous to mention. The Lord has power over them however, and will not permit them to invade the minds or the realms of innocent people.

In a good spirit realm however, there are many good things going on. The two realms are like night and day, literally. Is there is a realm in the middle though where both good and evil spirits roam. Yes. That realm is our own earthly realm and one of the reasons we are here is to learn to discern goodly things from evil things during our mortal lives and act accordingly. This is our earthly realm and it is a probationary state.

> *"nevertheless, there was a space granted unto man in which he might repent; therefore this life became a probationary state; a time to prepare to meet God; a time to prepare for that endless state which has been spoken of by us, which is after the resurrection of the dead.*
>
> *- Alma 12: 24 (Book of Mormon)*

> *"For behold, if Adam had put forth his hand immediately and partaken of the tree of life, he would have lived forever, according to the word of God, having no space for repentance; yea, and also the word of God would have been void, and the great plan of salvation would have been frustrated.*
>
> *– Alma 42: 5*

The spiritual knowledge I speak mainly of in this essay though is benevolent knowledge, (good) rather than malevolent knowledge (evil). That 'good' knowledge is gained gradually and mainly by asking our

Creator to supply us with correct information in His own way. It is my experience that He will accommodate us in that wish. It is also fitting for us to give thanks to Him when the results come in.

Thus, it is required on our part to study the scriptures and even experiment on 'the word'. 'The word' I refer to here is the word of God according to the Bible, and in my case, the Book of Mormon as well, which I consider to be a second witness of Jesus Christ.

Because you are reading this book, I will assume you readers are thinking adults with noble ambitions, and that you are curious, or perhaps eager to gain as much knowledge as you can about how to access the good Spiritual realm of which I speak.

That good Spiritual realm is beyond the realm of science, as we presently understand the word. Thus, I say that verification of that realm is difficult to document, therefore, the best way to verify it is to seek it out and then feel the influence of it in your mind and even in your soul.

Also, we know little about spiritual realms because they are not material realms and science, as we know it today, is concerned <u>only</u> with discernable matter and solid data. Often though, we can sometimes witness those ethereal realms when we are in a dream like state where spirits or spiritual images can drift in and out of them.

This is not always safe however because the spirit realm could include supernatural influences. In any case, we should be cautious when we seek information about that good realm because, as I say elsewhere in this book, demons can be masters of disguise. The devil has taught them well in the fine art of acting and theater.

How will we know the reality of these spirits I speak about? Firstly, we must study it out and ponder it from all angles, mainly the scriptural angle. The ball is in our court. Secondly, we must ask again for a spiritual witness of it by the Holy Ghost, as to whether or not it is real and true.

Demons or evil spirits can be persuasive, even in the ethereal world of night dreams. However, they are not always successful at that. They can pretend to be our pals. Most well bred people however, are particular about who they want to be their pals. Some spirits can even pretend to be innocent victims themselves. That is so they can gain our sympathy or even just gain our acceptance of them as impotent and innocent beings. But they are not innocent and they are not impotent. They are, in fact, skilled actors and actresses who use subtlety and charm to achieve their ends when they are given that opportunity in your dreams. Thus, be careful about letting them perform for you at all, even in 'bit parts'.

When I begin to awaken and find myself subjected to unpleasant narratives, images and circumstances, I will recoil, but even when I recoil, I have noticed that there is still a residue of ugliness that remains and I will need to focus on a higher principle so that I an get back to normal. Those higher principles are always there, but they need to be recalled so that we can be aware of those things. Personally, I keep a catalogue of good thoughts and favorite scriptures of mine on my desktop. I can always turn to those for a healthy diversion.

The president of the Church of Jesus Christ of Latter Day Saints, Russell M. Nelson, has said that in these latter days if a person does not seek the Spiritual guidance of the Holy Ghost, they will not survive these latter days intact.

I realize that dream scenarios are not of my own making, thus, I may not be responsible for their presence, but I am responsible when I invite those tricksters and their images to linger in my mind and cause trouble or worries or temptations.

In any case, we must all be mindful of the context that we live our lives in. I could go on and on, but let me just say that the Bible advises us to 'stand in Holy places'. A holy place might be a temple or a good church, but it also might be a warm home where the people in it are capable of being kind and loving to the other people who live there.

CHAPTER 6

Seek True Messages in Your Mind

God is a God of truth and therefore, a God of reality. Reality is a permanent thing. It will always be there. Reality is good and bad. It will be up to us to decide which direction that we will let reality take us. All things in life are fleeting except for things of the spirit. The messages of the Holy Spirit are sanctified and true. Therefore, they can be trusted. The Holy Spirit is a guardian of truth, but not of lies or fantasy.

Fantasies are mostly lies. They are lies that somehow make you feel good. That is where the deception lies. They are lies that are mostly lies about having physical pleasures and dreams of having power. There is no real affection in such lies, only foolhardiness. Human power cannot be gained in reality, other than in our fantasies, exept by hard work and righteous dedication.

That is because God is always present in reality and His angels are watching us and they report their findings to Him. God never lingers in Satan's realm except wen it is expedient to try to persuade us with His gentle voice to follow His ways. He does not produce extravagant advertising campaigns to try to convince us of anything. He knows that His words of truth are the only things that will lead us to an honorable and safe future.

In Satan's realm lies will rule. That can also include half-truths. That is the way he works. He creates illusions of reality that can entice and seduce naïve souls, but those ways only lead to bring about an illusion of reality. He accomplishes this by establishing bedrock of lies that might seem politically correct to inexperienced children and even some adults, but in reality, they are traps because their final goal is the enslavement of human beings as they become trapped by their own fantasies and their own lusts. People who are not entertain delusions will recognize this.

Satan is a tyrant. He wants everyone to worship him instead of worshipping God. Therefore, some people tend go to Satan's realm for a 'fix' or what they perceive as an easy way out. That might be easy to invoke, but it is also very dangerous.

In God's realm, God rules. His laws are plainly laid out for our benefit and anyone who violates those laws will do so at their own peril. Aside from those laws that He gave to humanity, He also has laws and truth that he reveals to people personally. These truths come in the form of revelations. That just means that they are truths that are being 'revealed' to us for our benefit. And what a blessing they are.

People like interesting stories. Stories provide them with an escape from their problems. Satan is a storyteller. He is also a moviemaker. His movies have lots of drama. Most people like drama. Some people are addicted to drama. Fear has some drama within it, so does adrenalin. That is why those things make effective tools for nefarious purposes.

The devil is crafty. His realms are hidden much of the time, but they can still be attractive to unsuspecting and vulnerable people. A mouse click will be enough to open a file in his carnal realm. You might even have a personal memory of a file from your own past that is easily accessible for you. The devil knows this.

Sometimes, I forget to seek the light in the morning time. Yes, I can forget. I, who likes to see myself as a wise man, can be stupid enough to forget some things. In that way, I am wretched. The light is here now on this morning however, and I am feeling good. I feel that I am resolved to resist any enticements, but must not be overconfident because I remember how enticements in the past have deceived me.

It is an acquired skill to spot the Holy Ghost amongst the bevy of Spam type messages that come into our minds from outside every day. To be able to say, 'There it is. That is what I need.' That signifies a true message to me from my Lord'. In this way I can differentiate a true message from the torrent of 'spiritual spam' that can fill up my spiritual folder.

That is the time when He is blessing you. He has been waiting for you to recognize that moment with your discernment, your intelligence and your ability to recognize things that are of the Spirit. That is a gift that should always be appreciated if you have it.

God monitors all the messages that we receive and transmit. When we ignore the true messages, God is not pleased and He might just signal the Holy Ghost to cut off the connection or 'hang up the phone', so to speak.

This might sound harsh, but it is fair game. Would you stay on the line talking to someone who wasn't listening to a word you said or who was reciting lies or gibberish? I say that we can always ask questions from God in prayer and He will often give us answers to those questions in His own way. We only need to be sure that we are not 'asking amiss'.

It is always a delicate state of mind when the Holy Ghost is near and we should be leery about making assumptions. I talk about becoming 'refreshed' elsewhere in this book. When you receive a message that you are reasonably certain is an inspired message from a higher level that is when you can become refreshed. Appreciate that message. Bask in it. Expand on it in your journal.

WARNINGS:

Don't Be Afraid Of Them. They might frighten you, but remember that the Truth will Only Be For Your Good.

A part of a person's preparation to receive revelations involves the acknowledging of warning signs, both of danger or of any immoral influences that might be nearby. Such warnings or influences are things that can throw you off your path from reaching your righteous goals.

For example, it is shameful if we should picture in our imagination good and respectable women taking part in such things as pornographic acts. That twisted perspective can change a man or a woman's life from a heavenly and pleasant state into some bizarre and immoral narrative whose perceptions originate directly from hell.

I must explain it in that way so I can describe with clarity the way in which filthy thoughts can stop a person's righteous trajectory right in its tracks and send that person scurrying around like a rat in a maze so that they cannot find a safe place to hide.

C H A P T E R 7

Temptations and the Last Pratfall

I was recently reflecting on my career in the music business over the last fifty years or so. Around 1978 I finished my job with a show band. It had lasted about five years and was, all in all, quite successful.

I was then thinking about starting my own band, but I needed to decide whether I wanted to go into the 'A' nightclub circuit, which was mostly pop/rock stuff which I did not feel comfortable with, or I could go into the B circuit which was mostly a country bar circuit which was more 'down to earth'. I wasn't really the spandex type and I preferred songs of a country nature, so I decided to go the country route. One of my talents was writing songs that had lyrical substance to them. Country music, in general, had more of that substance at that time, in my personal opinion, so that is the musical area that I chose to go into into.

Hence, I started exploring some of the bars on the country circuit. Some of the bars were fairly respectable, but some were not. In any case, I felt I needed to play most of them if I was going to be able to keep the wolf away from my door.

One night I went to one of the seamier bars in Winnipeg to take a look around. I noticed it was a pretty wild place and even though I was not too religious at the time, the word 'sinful' popped into my head at some point when I was in that room. I guess I had always thought about the devil's influence in any wild situations where self-control was not a factor in people's behavior. I wondered about the overall morality and immorality of the whole bar scene.

I remember noticing one woman there who was in a happy semi-drunken state as she flitted around the room making contact with a number of people. I got the impression that her life in general was not a stable one. That attitude was not confined to that one woman. It was everywhere I looked and it was spurred on by the noise and the loud music in the room. A spirit of decorum was nowhere to be found.

I don't like to judge others, but I have always known that there are many traps out there in the world. The world of booze, drugs and sex was a likely place for a person to experience a trap of some kind. Those bits of cheese can look pretty good to a hungry mouse, or a hungry man. Personally, I wanted to avoid any and all traps, so I just made a point of observing things that night and I did not get personally involved in the rush to find something outside of myself that might cause me to become excited.

Despite the fact that I considered myself streetwise, I should have known that I was not totally impervious those kinds of influences. That bar on a Friday night was a place where people could lose their inhibitions easily. So I asked myself how evident was the devil's actual influence on people in such a bar on a Friday night. Was it a Satanic influence that actually influenced men and women to pursue sexual sins?

I had a thought enter my mind then that I think was a bit of a revelation or an epiphany. I got a feeling that, no, Satan wasn't really causing the people to sin. The people were doing it all by themselves. They didn't need Satan's help.

Satan had set things in motion a long time ago and the people there were degrading themselves on their own out of habits that had been formed in the past. And it was all in the name of FUN. Everybody likes to have fun. Right?

If Satan was there, I imagined he probably wouldn't be doing anything except sitting back and watching what was going on. And laughing. And cheering.

He was watching the people do it to themselves. They drank their booze, they took their drugs, and later maybe some had sex. But mostly the higher things in life, like the contemplation of God for one, were quite irrelevant. That factor of 'totally ignoring God and His will' was probably habitual on their part, but I figured that other people's problems were not really my business and I soon left the place.

I never forgot that experience, but I never really examined that way of thinking because, basically, I knew I wasn't smart enough to figure it all out. That is, until many years later when I became much more learned in the gospel and did more reflecting on God and the devil and the human condition.

So, years later, as I pondered that same event again. I came to the conclusion that my original impression was probably right. The devil didn't need to 'spur' people on. They were doing it to themselves. The devil, if he was there, was just laughing. And cheering.

He set the whole thing in motion a long time ago. He doesn't make us do anything wrong. He doesn't need to. We entertain him with our foolish behavior and our foolish beliefs and our total lack of discernment. Thus, I would say that we are his personal, and willing, 'clowns'.

He doesn't really hate us that much simply because we don't matter to him. He doesn't care if we live or die. Hating people who don't matter takes too much energy for him. We are simply not worth it and so are of no concern to him. He wants to seduce people of intelligence and integrity, not weaklings. Weaklings are a piece of cake to him and offer him no real challenge. It is God's brightest children that he desires to seduce. That is because he figures that that hurts God the most and that is the devil's main purpose to hurt God. He has also proven himself to be quite capable of that, or sohe thinks.

Yes, Satan hates the Father more than anyone because the Father expelled him from heaven a long time ago and would not let him, nor his minions, back in. Back then Satan wanted to rise above the Father and steal the Father's honor, but the Father would not let him do it, and instead He designated the firstborn Son, known as Jesus the Christ, to bring forth the heavenly plan on the earth. Jesus actually volunteered to do that to fulfill the will of the Father. *(Isaiah 6: 8)*

Satan hurts us because he thinks that by hurting us, <u>he is hurting the Father</u>. About Christ, the Book of Mormon says that:

> *"he cometh into the world that he may save all men if they will hearken unto his voice: for behold, he suffereth the pains of all men."*
>
> *- 2 Nephi 9:21*

The Father might be dismayed at our behavior because He loves us. That is no secret. The Father perhaps feels pain when His spirit children (us) suffer because of our own actions, like when we degrade ourselves and pursue our clownish activities.

The devil loves to laugh. His court jesters and clowns (us) make him laugh when we give in to the temptations that he set in motion a long time ago. He laughs because he knows that we clowns embarrass the Father.

The Father can withstand the pain however. He can do that because:

1. He has honor and Satan does not.
2. God has a physical presence in the world, as well as a spiritual presence, and thus, He is more powerful in both the physical world and the Spiritual world.
3. Most importantly, the Father has Eternity on His side. Satan does not have that. God knows that Satan will eventually perish.

Satan knows that too, but for Satan, being a spiritual bully is just as important as personal exaltation. In fact, he probably sees it as the same thing. We humans need to get to know though, in a basic way, the nature of Eternity, even just a little bit. We do that by getting to know the Father as well as we can. One thing we must realize is that the Father is Eternal, or as He has called Himself, 'Endless'. (Doctrine and Covenants 19: 41)

Even if we get to know Him a little bit at first, that should set us on our way with confidence and, hopefully, a certain amount of faith. A fullness of the knowledge of the Father will come in time when we learn how to perfectly discern things, and when we come to understand our own 'clown ship'. Hopefully, when we come to know the extent of that clown ship and its accompanying dishonor, we will then decide to eliminate it from our lives so that it will no longer be a part of us.

As Satan himself begins to perish, he will try to attract attention by doing clownish things himself, imitating some shenanigans he has witnessed in the mortal world. He knows what works best for his purposes. Satan's followers might find them funny, but the followers of God, who have gained the quality of discernment, will find them obscene. They will dismiss the devil and dismiss his antics and that will cause him to rant and rave as he runs down the road to oblivion.

When we realize that we mean absolutely nothing to the devil, but mean a lot to the Father who created us, we will cheer the devil's demise and we will rejoice in the sustaining of the Father.

When we give up on the devil and subsequently, on our clown ship, we will be giving up any desire to please the devil or to please any of the other clowns in his circus. Personally, I know that there was a time when I took a few clownish pratfalls for his amusement, but the Lord has remained close to me and I have, over time, had a change of heart and eventually, I decided to stifle my clowning ways and my pratfalls, and just be a friend to mankind in a more humain way.

To give up the devil, we might need to do combat with him. The devil doesn't like to lose followers. It is not that difficult to give up on Satan though, once we see how flawed he is. One of our main weapons in combating him is the weapon of ignoring him. A fire burns because it has oxygen to burn. <u>The oxygen that the devil requires to burn, or to do damage, is our attention</u>, even the attention we give him in our wicked imaginings. When there is no oxygen to be burned, a burning fire will extinguish itself.

The fire will only be reignited if we should desire to, once again, chase one of the many brightly colored lures that the devil has cast into the waterways of the world.

The devil does not have a body. Thus, he will not be able to counteract our inaction of ignoring him because he cannot physically act on us. He cannot hurt us as long as we have patience and refuse to fight him on his terms. If we fight him at all, it will be on our terms. The Father will watch our backs on this if we have courage and invite Him to assist us.

Our courage involves committing ourselves to receive of the Father's love and help. That will be available to us if our hearts and minds are in the right place. We will become more worthy of receiving God's love when we invite other people to come and partake of that same love in the same spirit that it was given unto us.

Partaking of the Spirit is a matter of our willingness. 100%. God would never force Himself on us. God watches and waits. He waits until we are finished our clownish antics, that He was never amused by, and then when we are ready, He will present Himself to us in all solemnity. He refuses to be a part of the clown act. As we dismiss our own clownish antics, we must also escape the circus itself. If the circus is still in our presence, we will be hampered in our abilities to perceive our God's presence. Images and memories of the circus will be too distracting for us.

Thus, we must turn away from the circus. That would include turning away from things like social media for example. In some instances a person may emerge from watching a Facebook site that may indeed be able to convey a small amount of knowledge to us, but we may not be able to receive any true wisdom because it will be mixed in with other things, like receiving the other clowns and the numerous freak shows that are in the circus. It becomes a matter of context and different contexts have different variables in them. Some of those contexts may involve things that we are familiar with and some that we are not familiar with and thus can make us, in our ignorance, eager to learn about them.

Aside from turning away, we must express a desire to be recognized by our God and be recognized by the Holy Spirit. We seek approval from our maker and it is a serious and heart felt desire. We do that through prayer. There is no other way we can express our desire to be recognized by the Spirit other than by just coming right out and asking for it.

If an unwise child runs away and joins the circus, he, or she, will soon be swallowed up in the circus way of life. They will seek to entertain others by learning routines from the other clowns and learning attitudes from the ringmasters and learning how to get attention from the people who run the spotlights.

Entertaining for money may be acceptable in some cases, but if those people do have talent, they will usually ignore the prime source of their talent, which is, in a way, a betrayal of the 'gift giver'.

"All things which are good come of God."
- Moroni 7: 12

Nothing bad can come from God. Warnings of bad things can come from God, but those things are not bad in themselves. Some of those warnings I call 'reverse revelations'. I will give you one example of that. I do believe however that the good Lord wanted me to experience a valuable perception that could be called the perception of 'contrast'.

One night I was in my bed and I couldn't sleep. I may have been having idle thoughts that day. I don't really remember, but I was feeling down emotionally and mentally and spiritually. I had no good feelings and I had no ambition. I even had a lack of hope. It was a sad situation. I might as well say that I would prefer to be dead if I had a choice.

So why do I say this was this some kind of revelation? I will tell you. I believe I felt the way I did because God withdrew His Spirit from me. Totally. When He did that, I, somehow, gained the perspective of <u>contrast</u>.

I knew at that moment that wickedness and loneliness was not a part of who I was. I remembered what it was like to previously feel the Spirit and it was a delightful memory. At that moment, I knew what it was like to <u>not</u> feel of the Spirit. It was ugly and I wanted desperately to get the Spirit back.

I felt like a bum, a beggar, a pathetic clown. That is how I perceived myself when I was without the Holy Spirit in my life. I soon fell asleep. I woke up in the morning feeling all right, but I did not forget the previous night when I did <u>not</u> feel all right. I did not forget what it was like to be without the Spirit.

I got out of bed and said a prayer. I noticed that I began to feel better already. I wrote in my journal about my experience I and did a self-appraisal at the same time. I decided to be more determined about living by gospel truths and reading scriptures and bringing good cheer to people around me, and going to the temple, and staying away from all harmful influences.

Over the next few days, I began to feel much better. You might say I 'got my mojo back'. I was actually thankful that I had those bad feelings that night because I could see the contrast between living with the Spirit and living without it. I had learned something important about myself and learned about the importance of seeking the Holy Spirit. I think I also learned a few things about how the Father works.

If people who have been blessed in their lives do not acknowledge those blessings of contrast, then those people are ungrateful, knowingly or unknowingly. It is the same result in either case.

People will never be truly happy no matter how rich or powerful they might become. If a talented performer ignores a Godly influence or refuses to testify of God, or Jesus, then he, or she, is just another high priced, or low priced, clown, who is doing nothing to preserve the beauty of the Lord and protecting his nobility that is constantly attacked by evil forces. People who the general public finds appealing are appealing have a responsibility to use their influence and 'stand ready' to protect the name of God from being sullied.

People who set themselves up as critics of God do so by setting themselves up as 'minor Gods' This does no good for anyone because those minor Gods, or swindlers, will always fall short in the end. When someone falls short under a spotlight, it is much more wicked than falling short in their own private space. This principle applies to the media and the circus that is sometimes called 'show business', and even applies to our social circles whether at work, school, or anywhere.

As I write these words, I am drawing attention to myself right now by making bold statements in a book that I hope will be read by the general public at large. So am I a clown? I don't think so because if I do ever boast of anything, I am never boasting or virtue signaling of myself, but I will boast of my God because I stand as a witness of the marvelous things He has done and will do. I have forsaken my clownship and so I now testify of the glory of the Godhead, who is the Father, the Son and the Holy Ghost, who are three separate Beings with one united purpose.

Also, as a member of the clergy, I feel I should warn people to beware of the devil's plan. His plan is to hurt us and our families and that can bring much sorrow to us. That is because when he hurts us, we feel guilty and begin to hurt ourselves. God might also feel pain in that case, but we can have faith that that pain will be short lived and God, in the end, will always emerge triumphant.

That pain weakens our spirit and causes it to shrink. It will also causes us to preserve certain devilish traps in our lives, traps which the devil presents to us, often in an attractive and/or entertaining way and or in a way where some adversary is pretending to be intellectually superior to us. His plan will be to try to persuade us to abandon our God in favor of another ideal, which doesn't actually even exist. That is the ultimate deception and it is designed specifically to hasten our own spiritual demise.

How do we combat that? There are four things we can do.

1. Pray often.
2. Obey the commandments.
3. Go to church. That is a true church that is witnessed by the Holy Ghost. You will learn a lot if you go to church with the right attitude. Even if you do not learn anything on one particular day, go anyways, if only for the reason that you will be in a place where you are supposed be, and as well, you will be, or should be, partaking of the sacrament there. Take pleasure in knowing that you are being obedient. Things will 'click' in in time. You will be blessed just for being in the place you are supposed to be. And I can witness that obedience pays off.
4. Take your last pratfall and then put away your clown wardrobe, for good. That will allow you to become a real and an honorable person; one who is loyal to our loving Father in Heaven.

CHAPTER 8

Seek for a Good Companion

(OR FINDING WARMTH IN A COLD WORLD)

SUBTITLE:
➲ **Deitrich Bonhoeffer**

I had some experience with religion when I was young. My Grandfather was the patriarch of the family and he was a staunch Christian and a member of the United Church of Canada. He was also a teetotaler and would not allow liquor in his house, which fits in perfectly with my own beliefs today.

My father was a professional musician and a bandleader and his attitude towards liquor was quite different from my grandfather's. My father played the piano and the vibraphones. He mainly performed in jazz venues and made a pretty big name for himself on the local Winnipeg music scene. My father, from my observations however, did not pay much attention to the advice that came from his father, nor did he share my grandfather's views on alcohol. My father was a fortunate man and he married a good woman who was a good wife and mother.

My mother did not attend church regularly, mainly for the reason that she didn't drive a car, but after I became converted to my church I studied the gospel and as I did I remembered some of the spiritual thoughts that my mother told me about as I was growing up. She spoke about many ideas that I had long forgotten about, but they often came back into my memory as I investigated the theology of my church.

I realized that she must have gone to church as a young woman and as well, she must have picked up some valuable truths from the church or from her own parents, because I knew that she had some wisdom and that she was a very spiritual woman.

If a man or a woman wants to be a happy person and a good spouse, I think it is vital that they somehow pick up a code of ethics along the way, a code that allows for the presence of self-restraint and self-discipline and also for humility. I'm not saying that Christianity is the only way to do that, but I will say that, for me, it was the most obvious way for me and the and the most rewarding way.

Marriage has its challenges. Some are big challenges and some are small challenges. Some seem to be actually insurmountable challenges and that is where trouble, like escape mechanisms and betrayals, can begin. The key to solving those problems is simple. I mean that they are simple to state, but are not often easy to accomplish. The key is simply to show love and to be kind to others, especially the ones you love, and do that as often as you can. Being busy and hard working may be good things, but they are not good excuses for withholding kindness and love.

To accomplish this attitude of kindness, I feel that there will be a need to accept a definite moral code into your relationships. Christianity, as it is explained within a sensible church, is my preferred method to get that moral code instilled in me and in those around me. It causes me to want to be good to others and to present ourselves as younger brothers and sisters of Jesus Christ Himself.

The reason why a moral code is so important is because it applies not only to one family or a married couple, but it also applies to a whole community of like-minded people. I am talking mainly about a faith community where common values are shared. This is very important in settling disputes and even in discarding any false principles that people in the community might erroneously tend to accept. This is why it is important to have a charter of some kind, or 'articles of faith' written by an acknowledged leader. This is so that people can refer to those main points of doctrine and make their beliefs clear so that there will be no misunderstandings.

So I think that the ideal goal for a community or a congregation should be for everyone to accept truth, love, patience, long-suffering, and the idea that sacrifice is always the ultimate example of those things. I say that these principles are, or should be, some of the main parts of a Christian doctrine.

If there are any younger people reading this I would highly recommend that they check with older people, older people whose judgments you can TRUST. When we dated there were certain standards that not as many younger people pay attention to these day. I am talking about sexual standards like making it clear, whether you are a boy or a girl, that you are in favor of <u>not</u> having sex before marriage and having a potential mate meet your parents and get to know them, and not watching inappropriate movies, etc. etc.

Please don't think of 'courting rituals ' as old fashioned ideas from another era. In fact, they are only common sense when you think of the risks that casual sex presents to you. Make sure that any potential mate knows your standards and understands the reasoning behind them before you make any commitments.

Another big part of Christianity is diligence and making covenants with God. In my church we call it 'walking the covenant path'. Baptism is one kind of covenant. It is making a promise that you will try your best to abide by cautious rules. Who would not want a potential mate to abode by such rules? It is not a guarantee, but it definitely increases your odds of finding true 'marital bliss' as opposed to finding future 'marital discord'.

Partaking of the sacrament is another important covenant. In my church, doing ordinances for relatives who have passed on is a way that we can allow them to partake of sacred covenants as well. We believe that the spirits of our dead ancestors are cognizant of what is going on and they wait eagerly for the time when they can partake of those ordinances and when many good things will be taught to them, and even taught to them by angels.

In the book of Matthew, Jesus spoke about making covenants. He said:

"For whether two or three are gathered in my name, there am I in the midst of them."

- Mathew 18: 20

Thus, we have His promise that when we witness a marriage ceremony or partake of the sacrament of the bread and water, or any other sacred ordinance, and do so in His name, then His spiritual presence will be in the room with us. Thus, if His words are true, we will be in the actual presence of Holiness every Sunday. That is why I say that I say that Marriage covenants are sacred to all concerned.

Speaking of kindness, the bible says that we mist be careful about how we speak to our loved ones and careful about the things we say. Depending on the situation and the people involved in it, a verbal attack on another person can do even more harm than a physical attack.

"But the tongue can no man tame; it is an unruly evil, full of deadly poison. Therewith bless we God, even the Father; and therewith curse we men, which are made after the similitude of God. Out of the same mouth proceedeth blessing and cursing. My brethren, these things ought not to be Doth a fountain send forth at the same place sweet water and bitter?"

- James 3: 8-11

If there are any young people out there looking for a good partner or spouse, I would suggest that they seek out a person who has a lot of integrity. If you do that, there is a good chance you will love them for the rest of your life. If you are attracted to someone because of looks or money or personality flares, there is a good chance that those things will wear thin after awhile.

Dietrich Bonhoeffer

Dietrich Bonheoffer was a German priest during the Second World War. He denounced Hitler many times and was eventually executed by the Gestapo for allegedly supporting the removal of Adolph Hitler. I mention him here because he once said something about the sacred institution of marriage. He believed that marriage was a divine ordinance and a law that came from God. He knew that God's laws were much wiser than the desires of young people who believed on the unproven power that love should have in a relationship.

It was said that he once told a young couple wanting to get married something to the affect that –

> *"Love is a wonderful thing, but love can be supplanted over time. You think that love will always sustain your marriage, but that is not really true. In fact, it is your marriage that will sustain your love."*

CHAPTER 9

The Good, The Bad and The Refreshed

Life can be complicated. It involves both good and bad things. There are also some mixed attitudes, ideas, people and principles that contain a measure of both good and bad. There is a saying that goes:

"All it takes for evil to prevail is for good men to do nothing."
- E. Burke

You may have read this maxim many times, but nonetheless, the reason that ideas become oft-repeated maxims is probably because the principal is true. Thus, I am talking about three basic factors in society. The 'good' people could be divided into two kinds. There are good people who do nothing and so are pretty much useless. Then there are, those good people who actually do something to show that they are sincere in their honorable goals. Those are the people who make a difference. They are always, or should be, motivated to do some hard work and approach that work feeling refreshed and ready for the work.

There also bad people in the world. Some of those bad people are intentionally bad and some if them are not intentionally bad but are pretty much ignorant about the damage that they cause by their bad decisions.

That takes into account the refreshed among us. I don't know exactly how those people became refreshed, but you will know them when you hear them speak. So I ask, what is the catalyst that enables a person to feel refreshed?

> *"A person might feel refreshed when they are working on a hot day and have a big cool drink of water, but that is minor compared to when you are feeling down on the world, and you are given given a good dose of truth by a faithful servant of God."*
>
> *- P.W. Doodle*

People need to find ways to 'refresh' themselves in order to become motivated. For some men and women that motivation might come naturally. For most people though, especially those facing pernicious forces and enemies, there needs to be some specific means of becoming motivated. Receiving spiritual refreshment always begins before any healing can take place. It begins when you take on a personal challenge and you are up to that challenge. You can really only be up to that challenge when you have actually worked on establishing good values in your character.

In other words, the healing comes firstly by obeying the commandments. That might come naturally for some people, but not for everyone. To keep the commandments, we must first <u>know</u> for certain what God's commandments consist of. That 'knowing' will only come to us by study, prayer, church attendance, keeping good company, etc. Thus, that will be your "cool drink of water on a hot day.

A belief in God or a belief in a set of good values is one thing that can set the stage for people to feel a desire to do good and productive things. If that involves a confirmation of wisdom on your beliefs then all the better. I am simply stating that, personally, I love good things and I admire people who do good things. How about you? Is that a realm that YOU would want to be a part of?

The values of such people will always be seen to rise above the values of lethargic people, and of course, actual evil doers. The positive motivation that will always be provided by higher powers (the water givers in a sense) and will, become evident to the practitioners of them, and even to people who witness the good results that come from them. I don't want to state the obvious here, but I have met criminals and swindlers and have been victimized by them a few times in my life. I want to avoid any such occurrences in the future and at all cost.

Lots of people may be good people, but how many of those good people are <u>refreshed</u> people and are that way consistently and so are usually agreeable to become enthusiastic about doing good things? I don't know the answer to that question. I only know that we can be effective in attaining our desires when we have a good heart and when see things clearly. That means when we see things from a 'whole perspective'.

People should be 'whole' in their beliefs and hold nothing back. A whole person should be a motivated person or a person who is able to 'refresh' themselves with the truth, a truth that is hopefully, somewhere present in their belief system. They do that with what might be called the 'balm of truth' which is a healing procedure that comes from biblical times.

That is when the Holy Spirit will gives us access to Him in our most solemn moments when we ask for it in the name of the most Holy thing we know. If we don't know what is Holy, I suspect we will be unlikely to get an answer. I suspect then that that will become our first priority of study, for the Lord does not hold ignorance or laziness as an excuse for inaction or lethargy on important issues.

So how many people believe strongly in righteousness and are willing to stand up for, and fight for principles that promote that? How many are active in the promotion of goodness and justice ruling in our society? That is as opposed to people who are basically asleep at the wheel and think that someone else will take care of the various injustices and the messes that we hear about every day?

How many people are refreshed enough so that they will not let their courage fail and will hold on tight to the ideal of a fair and just society? When I speak about justice, I speak about 'true' justice and not the justice of narcissists or virtue signalers who belief in exterminating any other man or woman who has a different opinion than they do. How many men or women will be motivated to stand up and defend the people who are exploited or bullied by certain tyrannical and greedy people who populate certain areas of this planet?

Sometimes people talk about 'holistic healing'. That is the idea of becoming balanced in every aspect of our character and/or our personality and letting that work for us. A chain is only as strong as its weakest link so let us apply that idea to ourselves and concentrate on the positive intensely while, at the same time, being open to the possibility of any 'positive change' that might be of benefit to us.

We should not have fragmented desires that cause us to become disorientated or confused or to 'hold back'. Personally, I tend to see things from a spiritual point of view. My will should be in harmony with the will of our Creator Himself, as much as is possible.

The scriptures say we should have "an eye single to His glory". *(Doctrine and covenants 4: 5)* Also, the first commandment in the Bible commands that we should "love God with all thy heart, might, mind and strength". That is the ultimate example of having an eye single to His glory.

Does this mean that we will need to be 'perfect' in our servitude to the Lord? No. Too often we feel inadequate in speaking for our great Creator and tend to 'back off' because we are aware of our unworthiness as fallible human beings. Brother Bradley R. Wilcox recently gave a talk in a church conference in October of 1021. It was entitled "Worthiness is not Flawlessness'.

He said that we may all be unworthy, but the Lord does not expect us to be flawless. He knows we are not flawless, but if we are sincerely trying our best to fulfill our righteous duties then that is enough. He gave the example of a young man who confessed to one of his leaders, "maybe I should just stop coming to church. I'm sick of being a hypocrite.

His leader said to him, "You are a hypocrite if you lie about it, or try to convince yourself that the church has the problem for maintaining such high standards. Being honest about your problem and taking steps to move forward is not being a hypocrite. It is being a disciple."

I was talking to some contemporaries this week during Sunday School about this subject. We generally agreed that it can be easy for the average person to 'get down' on themselves and harbor thoughts about our own inadequacy or harbor memories of past failures. As I listened to people's contributions to the conversation, I realized that the main point in we needed to focus on was <u>not</u> to perform our duties perfectly, but it is <u>how</u> we might become '<u>refreshed</u>', even every day. This is so we can come as close as we can to Him.

What a joy that would be! Our own diligent faith would be a vital factor in our success. That means that we would have no doubts that we are quite capable of becoming better people.

What was the solution that we all decided upon at that meeting? We decided to get back to the basics of the gospel IE: Prayer and pondering, the partaking of the sacrament, doing service for others, etc. We saw those things as a means of becoming refreshed in the Spirit.

Those things are all necessary components of a good motivational program that would give us the focus that we needed in order to become better, more holistic, more productive and happier people. In short, get in touch with your Maker on a personal level and just try to do things the way that He would do them. That will be enough.

Does doing good deeds leave us open to be accused of being called a prude or a 'goody two shoes'? If it does, so what? If something works for you, then use it. Let your good intentions actually work right up until the end. People are going to think what they want to think anyways, and with some of those people, perhaps even many, there will be absolutely no room for opposing thoughts on any matter.

That is why it is so valuable to have good friends or even acquaintances, who are solid in their beliefs and honest in their desire to take a righteous stand on issues without presenting an air of superiority. Thus I say, do whatever it takes to face the day with clarity of purpose, while being aware of people who would try to 'rain on your parade' or throw a 'monkey wrench' into whatever project you choose to be working on.

There are people who would do that. Those people can be dealt with in various ways, but the first thing you must do is be articulate enough and courageous enough to let them know that you are wise to them and that you will refuse to be pushed around by them, intellectually or otherwise. Thus, I would recommend that you ask yourself, 'What would be something that would cause you to become spiritually refreshed today?'

Cynical people usually have theatrical personalities. They like to perform for others and they like to play the devil's advocate, but they are rarely deep thinking or articulate in an honest way. Thus, we should learn to talk their language if you must, and you will find away to use their own words against them. That can bring a rewarding feeling to you when you can successfully do that without offending them. And with some practice, it is not really that difficult a thing to do.

CHAPTER 10

Motivation 101

SUBTITLES:

➲ Pointless Legacies = Pointless Lives

Allow me to ask you a personal question. What drives you? What inspires you? What motivates you to get up in the morning and go to a job that is compromising, at best, and involves hard work that allows you little time to do the things that you really want to do? What moves you? What propels you? Take time to think about it if you need to.

We both know that I will not be able to hear your answer because I am on the other side of this book in a mutual time/space warp (a rather inconvenient situation), but I assume that you have some sensible and valuable motivating forces behind all of the things that you do.

Sometimes we do not have any interest in the things that other people direct us to do. In my case, attending high school was an example of that. I was quite bored with it. As well, later on, sometimes we lose interest in the things that we have chosen to do in life; our jobs, for example.

I do not think that those feelings of disinterest are necessarily common because surely are there some other, more positive or passionate reasons why you do the things that you like to do. Or do you just do things out of a sense of duty or obligation with little or no enthusiasm?

To some people this question does not really matter. They are quite content with who they are how their lives are going and they need no outsider to cast doubts on their personal state of well being and I say that I sincerely congratulate them on their satisfied state and wish them well. But given the rates of suicide, divorce, violence, crime, single parent families, abortions, international tensions, and general unhappiness in the world, I think that there are many people who have need to ask themselves this question on a regular basis so that they might monitor all situations and try to remedy those ones in which they find their personal happiness quotient lacking. We all need to ask ourselves from time to time if we are on the right track or if we could use some kind of well thought out correction.

This following prayer fits that perfectly:

"God grant me the serenity to accept the things I cannot change, the courage to change the things I can change, and the wisdom to know the difference."

- The Serenity Prayer

Personally, I try to live by righteous principles. I am not without my own flaws and lazy tendencies, but nevertheless, I do believe that it would be ideal if all of us tried to live by righteous principles with the goal that we should all be as independent as we can be. These principles are not just words printed on a page. They are real and active. I have <u>decided</u> to try to incorporate these principles into my being to the point where they will actually become the motivating or the driving forces in my life.

Life is action. What is the most common form of self contained physical motion in nature? It is a circular motion, which is found in things like spirals and circles. What shape of object is most suited for movement in nature? It is a sphere, or a wheel, which is a part sphere. How does a sphere move? It rolls. It uses less energy because it's shape allows it to be less affected by friction. What initially propels it? It gets pushed an outside force of some kind. Its speed will depend upon whether it is pushed lightly or pushed strongly.

However a sphere may fare on an earthly plane, it will always tend to get worn down because of the natural forces of the earth, namely the friction that is caused by gravity. It also gets dirty as it picks up dirt and grit on its way.

I am making an analogy here. That is, what can we do as people to cause the sphere that is our <u>character</u> to move most efficiently and to rise above the dirt and grime of the earth? Also consider that our characters are of our own making and we do have the power to direct them or change them for good or for bad.

Pointless Legasies = Pointless Lives

Do some people just live pointless lives. I suppose that some, but everybody has their reasons for the things they do and I suppose that, in their own way, most people are trying their best. I may be one of the slackers, but I hope that I am not. History will be my judge in one sense. God will be my judge in a real sense. But as a human being who tends to naturally consume, and demands more than I produce or give, what good am I?

Even if we happen to be nice people and can display some sort of intelligence and we are reasonably kind to others, could all of those good character traits be just put into practice by us for reasons that are other than for our own self-interest?

So I ask the question, "Is there some kind of foundation that we can build upon to give us to allow our bodies to prosper in our lifetime and even have our souls enter into the eternities with a clean conscience that will perpetually sustain us?"

I have observed many people my own age display the attitude that their children and grandchildren are the things that give them the most pleasure in life. I say, "Good for them". But is that enough? Our children who are a generation below us older folks will eventually get caught up in their careers and in raising families and in their social lives. Those are good things, but they also take a lot of work and there is still a large learning curve involved for them. That is not their fault because they are new adults and are barely past the stage of being children themselves.

The older generation (people my age) should be the wisest generation, although that is not always the case. From my observations, many of my contemporaries seem to often hold their grandchildren as the apex of their existence. Sure, it makes sense to do things for them and it shows that we care, but what do we really give to those grandchildren that we care so much about? Do we give them money? Do we joke around with them? Do we show affection for them? Is that enough?

We may desire to become close friends with them, but really, that is not very realistic. Our grandchildren are experiencing the innocence of childhood and are, of necessity, in a place where older people cannot go. We can go there and look around, but we cannot reside in that place with them. Our access to the realm of childhood becomes more limited with time. Perhaps that is simply because we know too much.

Thus, it seems to me that the best thing we could do for our grandchildren and generations beyond, would be to teach them by word and by deed, <u>how to be happy</u>.

It is also important that we not make this process ego driven, or in other words, to not try to teach them to be like us. How do we do that when our own experiences in life might be somewhat limited? If our own experiences are limited, then it makes sense to me that we should live by strong principles that are taught to us by either the written word or the spoken word. They will be principles that we perceive to be in harmony with truth.

We don't want to constantly preach to them and we don't want to let them go off on their own like a lamb into a forest full of wolves. So we must find a balance between letting them make their own decisions and advising them of a sure path in life as far as we are able to discern that path ourselves.

To avoid letting our teachings becoming ego driven, we also need some kind of an exemplar from whom they can learn and maybe even a person who we can learn from too. That way we can learn together. I do believe that learning together is the best kind of learning. Thus, we might need an exemplar from outside of ourselves who is not driven by ego or by money or by blood allegiances or by race allegiances or by traditions.

To me, Jesus Christ fills that bill. The things that he did and said should be taught to everyone and taught <u>according to the correct knowledge</u> of who He was and why He came to earth. I have searched and have found no other exemplar that comes close to him in history or in world religions. The only other people I have come across who could serve as a great exemplar, are people who <u>actually use him as an exemplar.</u>

We should first teach our children and grandchildren five basic things to help them become happy and productive people. First, that they are loved by their creator and that they should always try to establish a connection to Him. They should also be taught that this could be a lifetime process.

Second, they need to be taught that they should have a purpose in life and, possibly, more than one purpose. It may not be clear to a parent or an adult what that purpose is at the present moment, or will be in the future, but they will have a lot of time to think about it. Hopefully, that will eventually become clear to them and, hopefully again, those desires will be accomplished by them according to the talents and the strengths that have been given to them.

Thirdly, they need to be taught how to be humble and how to get along with others. That involves being charitable, kind, respectful, and being civil or courteous.

Fourthly, they should be taught to be grateful. When we are grateful, we will be humble and will appreciate the gifts that we have been given in life, rather than feel resentment about the things that we perceive were not given to us.

Fifthly, we must teach them to appreciate freedom. This means the freedom that allows to us to make decisions that we believe will be good for us and for society as a whole without being hindered by outside influences like peer groups or schools or governments who like to manipulate people's moral beliefs through various rules and regulations be they spoken or unspoken.

There is another kind of freedom that they should be taught to embrace and that is the freedom to break away from following along a wrongfully chosen path. This might also be called the freedom to 're-think' important matters. This freedom releases us from the personal bondage of bad habits and of wrongful ways of thinking. Some people do not have that freedom to rethink. For example, I heard recently about a member of a criminal gang who decided to leave the gang. He thought that he was a free man by living outside the laws of society. He was eventually allowed to resign from the gang, but only after a vicious beating that left him with many broken bones. This may be one extreme example, but intimidation from others often takes away people's freedoms in many different aspects of life.

So I say that this is the greatest gift that we older people can give to our progeny. It is the establishment of righteous teachings and righteous traditions within our families. They will be traditions that should always be open to scrutiny, but are open to scrutiny not based upon cynicism or rebelliousness, but on principles of love, honesty, kindness, respect and other virtues.

This teaching process that I describe is largely a process of sacrifice. Having children, teaching them and taking care of their needs is a sacrifice, and a sacrifice can be one of time and energy and money and even of physical and mental strain. The thing that makes it all worthwhile is the knowledge that, in the end, a greater good will come of it all. To be able to offer proof of this, it will be good to leave a good legacy behind. To leave behind a good legacy will be done mainly by setting a good example.

CHAPTER 11

Maintenance Strategies and Dealing with Memories

A large part of the maintenance strategy will be to live the gospel every day and serve people who are in need whenever you can. Much learning can happen when you serve others. It can cause you to become more compassionate, and more honest, pure and thorough and it also helps you to see how false perception can directly affect another person and stop their progression in its tracks.

Receive the rewards of your studies in your mind and in your heart and in the love that you feel for any righteous person who you may know. That is how you gain a testimony or a knowledge of the truth. The Spirit of God will rest upon you if you are diligent in your studies and unafraid of any spiritual impediments or devious trials that come your way.

Ideally, you and I are, hopefully, always learning from our experiences. That learning should guide us as we proceed into our future. Where do we store and sort out the memories and images born out of our experiences, both good memories and bad ones? We store them in the memory banks of our minds.

Are those memory banks dependable for our higher purposes? No. We can be as selective as we want to be about our memories according to our passion, or lack of passion, for the truth. We can also be selective about our memories according to the weaknesses of our imagination and according to the weaknesses of our ego and our natural desires.

Exercising a selective memory can work for us when we want to have positive thoughts, but it can also work against us when we feel the need to justify our selfish actions by any means possible. Therefore, we must become accustomed to working with reality and even cold, hard facts. If we do not do that we will probably fall <u>victim</u> to deception of one kind or another. Nobody, outside of a few disturbed people, desires to be a victim.

This is a cognitive process that I am speaking about and the results of it can be good or bad depending on which values we will decide to hold as a priority. Will those be the good values of our higher self or the bad values of our lower self?

If we should we sift through our memories, using a sieve that has no extra large holes in it, that can confirm our noble individual purpose in life. Will this process take place within a secure situation? Probably not. Mortal life, without a connection to God, is not a secure thing.

As we shift through our memories with that sieve, our imaginations and egos can sometimes deceive us when we stumble across a particular event that bothers us. That might lead us away from the true explanation behind what actually happened. Perhaps we never were aware of what happened because of our lack of the understanding of all of the factors that contributed to the event.

When, and if, we come to learn the truth about what happened, we will need to contemplate the nature of those unknown forces. Exact clarity and truthfulness will be required in the process of honest self-analysis.

The solidness of the truths that we internalize will help to create the basic foundation of our character, and even determine an actual portion of our intelligence, that is, if a valuable truth is actually learned by your deliberation. In the final analysis, our new, more truth-based character will expand the scope, however slightly, of our 'higher self' in a temporal sense and, possibly, even in an eternal sense. The higher the degree of certainty we have in our knowledge, the higher will be our level of intelligence and capability and will ultimately, even determine the level of joy we can attain.

Another factor in this quest is one of value judgments about our memories. Some people think that memories are airy and innocuous things, or even dead things, and they think that recalling any random memory will not do us any harm. The fact is that if a certain memory we recall had to do with an intense emotional or sexual experience it can come back with full force and even have the effect of a 'kick of a mule' on us. This is especially true of people with vivid imaginations and people who can have a problem maintaining control over their imagination.

> *"For the natural man is an enemy to God and has been from the fall of Adam, and will be, forever and ever, unless he yields to the enticings of the Holy Spirit and putteth off the natural man and becometh a saint through the Atonement of Christ the Lord."*
>
> *– Mosiah 3:19 (Book of Mormon)*

Thus, I say that self-imposed behavioral restrictions, or self-discipline, will be necessary to promote the likelihood of success, and therefore, the achievement of personal happiness.

That is where the 'short cut' of faith comes in. We will need to have a certain amount of faith in an active and loving Creator who can provide us with sanctification, mentally, physically and spiritually. That will provide us with a safe haven on our perilous journey in this fallen world. It will equip us to face trials with courage and other spiritual resources that we will need.

Some memories will be trifled with as we seek ways whereby we might entertain ourselves, but that inclination always takes away from the process of honest self-analysis. If certain memories and carnal images from the past should take hold in a person's psyche and excite us, they should be immediate and ruthlessly evicted so they do not diminish the solidness of a person's true self and their core beliefs. The eviction of such images should help us to bear hardships and trials in the future. Such trials may come upon us at some point in our life.

Good memories will become more apparent to us as we exercise the power of prayer. To do this we must inquire of God and seek a witness from the Holy Spirit of God as to their truthfulness. By utilizing this moral sieve we should be able to dispense with false or selective memories. Because those things can be difficult to understand, it might be more expedient to make a commitment, or a covenant, to just do the right things whenever we can. That is much more productive than self-justification or 'jumping to conclusions'.

Thus, this process is a steady one and a necessary one if we are to be successful in our very quest to achieve self-awareness. This is the main factor in what I spoke of earlier as 'receiving proper instruction'.

Three things that are most important in your life are: Who you are, what you do, and who you do those things with. Thus, keep in mind that who you do your "things" with will become a part of your personal realm. That is a risky thing to allow into your psyche

A church, good or bad, will present to you a realm. It should be a realm that is meant to house Holy things and Holy concepts and to facilitate holy ordinances like the partaking of the sacrament. This is even more meaningful when it is applied to a Holy temple that has been built and exclusively dedicated to the Lord. The influence of those Holy things has the 'ability' to actually expand itself to cover all of the events that happen in your daily life. Remember that.

Church, or any Holy place, is also a place that will, hopefully, facilitate the presence of the Holy Spirit or the Holy Ghost. All churches have some good people in them. This is evident by their sacrifices of time and money that good people give to good causes. Without those good men and women, I fear that I might not be strong enough to carry on the process of worship by myself. I need them. Granted, there may be a few hypocrites among the crowd, but in the end, those people won't matter. Nevertheless, a church should be for all people. That is why a church needs to be there be for a congregation, not just a lone person. The gospel is for all people, wise or not, virtuous or not.

I have a friend who said she did not attend church because there was too much dogma floating around there. I said that I did not like too much dogma either, but I did like good doctrine and sensible' doctrine. Some doctrines are better than other doctrines I have found. Personally I love the doctrine in my church, even though it is sometimes challenging.

If you feel a good spirit when attending a good church, know that you are in the place you need to be in. Knowing what church is the best one is a delicate subject. Nevertheless, some investigation into the doctrine of a church that appeals to you is good and should even be able to touch you in a deeper part of yourself. Thus, I suspect it might be better for a person to first find that 'deeper part of themselves' than to find that absolutely perfect doctrine that they hope someone will give to them.

CHAPTER 12

The Foundation of Faith

Nov. 28, 1990

I was thinking about some problems I was having in my life and I thought about my personal antidote that I have used in the past to overcome problems in general. It is of ultimate importance because it is the only name by which people like me can preserved in a state of peace, freedom and in some cases, joy. I am referring here to my personal testimony of Jesus Christ.

I was thinking about 'the cognitive abyss' that I fell into many years ago. It happened in April,1990, thirty years ago when I was a single parent and living in Winnipeg. It was the night before I was to be baptized at my church, a church that was very new to me.

I went to bed that night and I was monitoring my thoughts. I said a prayer before bed and I felt at some point during in my sleep that I was falling into an abyss, a dark hole of some sort. There seemed to be no end to that hole or to my fall. It was very disturbing and I felt a sense of hopelessness.

The night <u>after</u> my baptism, on May the nineteenth 1990, I said a prayer again, and I went to bed. I dreamed again that I was falling into that same dark hole, but this time it was different. After falling for some time, I felt that I hit something.

It was not a hard thing that I hit, but it was solid and it stopped my fall. It was ground of some kind that I landed on. It may have been rocks or it may have been fertile soil, or maybe both. I have no idea, but it was just there in that panacea of my mind and it stopped my fall immediately.

I knew I had landed on something and whatever it was it was something that was not there the night before. I knew instinctively though that it was something good. I could not explain what it was or even what it felt like. I just knew there was something there. That landing place also had a sign of life in it, or at least, there was something there that I felt was capable of preserving life.

In any case I was not a man without hope any longer. The perceived 'bottomless pit' that I fell into now had a bottom of some kind where I could once again feel a certain stability, and could even feel life itself.

Fast forward to this morning 9.00 A.M. Nov. 28. 2019. I was thinking about my testimony and my witness of the Spirit that I had gained over the years. I knew that my testimony was still there and had been there for the last thirty years.

I got out of bed, but I didn't feel very good. My body ached. So I went back to sleep. I woke up about an hour and a half later and I felt 100% better. It might have been that I was aware of my foundation again, but this time it was different than thirty years earlier. I was feeling bliss lines. It was a great feeling. My earlier feelings of discomfort had disappeared. I was feeling refreshed and ready for the day ahead.

I think it was because the vision I had on the night of my baptism came back into my mind and the message was still there. I figured that thirty years of gospel study entitled me to have that good feeling. In any case, my spiritual foundation had returned to me and returned in a in a better form than ever.

How did it do that? I didn't really do anything to instigate a foreign presence in my house on that morning, but something was happening to me, and in a good way. I was being acted upon, but I could not explain it perfectly, but you would need to read my past journal entries over the years to catch on to how I was feeling.

I felt like I had my testimony renewed. I thought about my brother David and was worried about him after hearing from another friend that his cancer tests were not successful. 'He needs to hear about this 'foundation of faith' that I experienced'. He also needs to hear about the importance of baptism, even baptism for the dead, by those in authority.

My brother and I were similar kinds of people as some brothers are. Despite our differing political opinions we were still fairly close to each other. He was, as opposed to myself, not interested in studying matters from a religious or a theological viewpoint. I wanted to tell him about the things that I had learned over time, but it was not easy because for one thing, he lived twelve hundred miles from me, and for another thing, it is not always easy to challenge another person's tightly held belief system, whether it was based upon a God or based upon some kind of secular/humanist philosophy. Most people can be very adamant about maintaining a belief system that they have held for literally decades, and for no good reason other than that.

My brother was a playwright, and a good one. The only problem with that as far as I could see, was that writers tend to see other writers as idols. Their philosophy gains purity only when it is found within the context of their own ideology It is the profession itself, the image of the starving artist that often has the most appeal. A man or woman who could express that eloquently was to be bowed down to in the world of the arts. All they needed was a few well-placed words and your contract was signed as an official literary guru.

"You are where it's at, Buddy. Even if you're a person with many personal problems like Earnest Hemingway, just sell your soul for a few good words and you can become an automatic Bohemian Guru."

I had been studying the scriptures for thirty years at that point and I had learned a great deal. I felt that I had some revelations over the years, but they were not the cataclysmic kinds of revelation where there was a 'rapture' that happened. It was more like a slow and steady progress. It was 'line upon line, precept upon precept, here a little and there a little' *(Isaiah 28: 10)*.

Those learning experiences were compounded over the years and led me to possess a secure testimony of spiritual things. A testimony like that could only come by the evidence of spiritual things being presented to me by an outside power, even a mysterious power. That is the way it happened with me.

December 26, 2021

My brother passed away ten months ago. On a personal note, a few weeks later, I heard his voice come to me in a dream. He only said two words to me. The two words were "Hey Brother." I only have one brother on the other side of the veil so I guessed that it was his Spirit talking to me. Somehow I thought that he might have some kind of message for me or a question or something else to say, but he didn't. There were no other words spoken by him.

I thought about it and I came to the conclusion that the afterlife can be a very vague and uncertain place, because the true authority has not yet been revealed there, not even revealed to the rookie ghosts and apparitions that are there who may have wandered into the Spirit world when their time was up.

There is a lot to learn there in the spirit world and I am sure that deceased people would have much more to say to loved ones, but if they have never been taught true principles about the divine rules that were necessary for living the 'real' good life, then uncertainty would be a major factor that they would need to deal with in the afterlife.

I'm sure they would want to say something more than 'Hey brother' or 'Hey sister', but for them the information they need will need to be divulged to them and divulged in proper context so that they will be able to understand it fully. The Lord knows that that is the way it should be done, but very few Bohemian Gurus actually know those things. These words are not to put a writer like my brother down. He was mostly a comedy writer and was able to bring smiles and laughter to the faces of thousands of paying customers. He had a special talent, but I don't think that he ever took himself too seriously as a sage or a seer, which was probably wise of him.

Learning about the way things actually work in the spirit world has not yet been made clear to the souls that go there and for the reason that they will simply not understand it without knowing the entire context of what was going on. They will eventually learn the truth about those rules and the details of them because they will be taught those things in higher realms.

Until that day arrives, uncertainty will still rule the day in the realm of unlearned spirits. The souls of the people in the higher realms will always need to be taught things though, because the things they needed to be taught were not covered in their initial classes at the local Seer school.

Indeed, the learned souls and spirits who have the authority and the wisdom to be able to help ordinary souls progress will teach them. Those good spirits will then be able to help the unlearned ones move onwards to higher forms of glory. In other words you could say that they will be 'taught by angels'.

Even if the unlearned souls manage to learn a few true principles, it can still be an uncertain learning environment because there are still a lot if unexpected factors in the big picture. As a philosopher once said, "a little bit of knowledge is a dangerous thing". Life, as well as relationships can be very complicated and exactness is not an option in the celestial kingdom of God. It will be a necessity.

I am saying that the learning that needs to take place firstly in the realm of the Spirit. The Spirit will then testify of the truth on people's minds. In the spirit world the learning will not necessarily be perceived as true if the learning cannot be traced back to the <u>source</u> of the learning. That means that all knowledge will needs to come directly or indirectly, from the Godhead, which consists of the Father, Son and the Holy Ghost, or even from the messengers who have the authority to speak for the Godhead.

Hence, I have come to the decision to have my brother to be vicariously baptized in the nearest Holy temple so that he can learn many things that did not take the opportunity to think about in mortality.

There are over one hundred temples on the earth and the people who are assigned to work in those temples have been ordained by worthy souls to do specific jobs there. Those jobs will need to be done for the sake of the freshly baptized souls who gather there and who will be overjoyed to hear their names mentioned as candidates for placement on the 'rolls of the faithful'. Those are the ones and who will be added to the list of the many who will receive vicarious baptisms and confirmations.

Not only that, but we are promised in the church that those souls who need enlightenment and intelligence will get it, assuming that they are sincere and humble and willing to pay the price of loyalty towards those righteous souls who have sacrificed much for us.

I must qualify my conjecturing by admitting that I do not know everything that goes on in those higher realms. I do believe though that, if I am somewhat accurate, those after death experiences will be great learning experience for those souls. Ones that will be comparable to no other experiences.

I can only hope that the false learning experiences that certain people acquired in this mortal world will not be too embedded in their characters. If they are 'embedded' then those souls might then be classified as 'incorrigible'. But I do not feel too sorry for them because, for the most part, they will be getting exactly what they wanted.

I say this because it is my belief that the hardest thing for people to do in this life is to get rid of bad habits and cynical attitudes that have become 'embedded' into their characters. Thus, it will take nothing less than their sincere repentance, and as well a compassionate act of God, to bring lasting healing to them.

It might also be noted that the stable-minded saints, those being the ones who have chosen the right path, will be granted a foundation underneath their feet so that they can gain traction and stability whenever they move and act on their beliefs. It is much easier for a person to 'shake something off' if they are standing on solid ground. Otherwise, they will just be 'twisting in the wind'. I pray that all honest souls will be able to plant their feet firmly on the ground when they accept the wonderful invitation to move forward to a better place.

As for me, I know not what the future holds. I do not know where I will end up. I do know of a surety though that I have been given a spiritual foundation underneath my feet from which I can speak the truth and stand strong for it. That is the most important thing that I know of in this world.

CHAPTER 13

Families and Parenting

I do not claim to be an expert on parenting. My parenting experiences have not been perfect and I also know that there are a lot of other parents who seem to do a fine job of raising their children without any help from me. Nevertheless, I make my observations because I know that it is such an important part of life, and it can also be a very complicated part of life, seeing as how all children have different personalities and needs. So I would now like to make some general comments on parenting on the basis of my experience and observations that I have made by watching others.

From the day a person leaves high school until they are in their fifties or sixties, their life will be a whirlwind as soon as they become parents. That 'whirlwind' phase that the majority of people experience begins with trying to find the right spouse and decide on a career they wish to pursue. Soon after that, in most cases, children come into the picture and things become very busy. That can get even more complicated when misfortune raises its ugly head. Things always get complicated when things like divorce happens, or if harmful behavioral habits should enter into the picture.

The point here, for parents, is that the whirlwind years will occupy most of your life and most of your thoughts and energy. Hopefully, people will take some time along the way to get their bearings and be able to look at child rearing as a great God-given privilege and not as a daunting, chore. A strong faith is the best thing to allow parents to maintain their original goals and the good desires for their family.

These days, there are evil forces in the world that want to <u>teach</u> our children that bad things can be seen as good things, that is if the perceptions taught and the priorities of things are taught according to an evil agenda. Some of these agendas can be a part of some false and dangerous doctrine. Sex education is a good example of how a certain false doctrines can be taught in the name of true doctrine. One way they do this is by appealing to the great secular Gods, who are the Gods of relativity rather than the God of truth.

When teachers teach innocent children about sexual matters they can easily fall into the trap of teaching them to 'tolerate' immorality, whether that is on purpose or not. These teachers are relative thinkers at best and ignorant, unprincipled thinkers at worst. The amazing things is that the many parents of these children, are too trusting and not aware about the precariousness of public education that gives teachers permission to 'preach' their secular religion to innocent children.

The bible refers to pornographers as 'purveyors of filth'. Can this description cross over into the realm of education in the form of 'sex-education'? I think that it can, and especially when the adults who establish the sex education curriculum are without morals themselves and can even be titillated by the whole bizarre and destructive process that they are given power over by their myopic administrators.

Some people regard family relationships as ultimate relationships. Not me. There is something that is more important than 'blood lines' and that is what I call 'spirit lines'. Spirit lasts forever. When you die you will be embalmed. Your blood will be drained and then washed down the sewer. Spirit, however, will last forever. Blood lines will not. Spiritual bonds then, are the ultimate bonds. As Jesus said when he was told His family was waiting to see Him when He was 'on tour':

"whosoever shall do the will of my Father which is in heaven,
the same is my brother, and sister and mother."
– Matthew 12:50

Public schooling, like it or not, is a socializing process orchestrated by the powers that be in the educational system, none of whom are perfect human beings.

Personally, I recommend home schooling to parents because of the educational wide-eyed ideologues and academic oligarchs that have infested the public education system in recent years. That is not to mention a smattering of sexual perverts and child abusers who call themselves 'advanced' who have joined ranks with them. In any case though, I worked in many public schools teaching music and creative writing and I can say that the good teachers far outnumbered the bad teachers.

As far as school administrators and policy makers go, that is another story, and if I was a parent with school aged children now, I would not hesitate to do some serious investigating as to the hidden social agendas of new administrators and even teachers. In any case, I also recognize that homeschooling is not always possible.

Morality is often linked with the teachings of sexuality. By that I mean some of the perverted notions that are taught by power hungry and self-declared enlightened teachers telling pupils that gender is not set and it can be 'fluid' if the pupil has become 'woke' like they are. Some teachers have been programmed by the powers of academia to think that the study of a sacred act like sex should be taught from a scientific point of view or even a non-judgmental and all-inclusive point of view, where it is okay to study various deviant kinds of sex and peak the curiosity of the young students. Such intellectual drivel is unacceptable in my world.

People may accuse me of being 'old school' but I don't care. There is definite right and wrong in my world and I think it is that way in everybody's world although some people have been successfully brainwashed by the so-called academic 'experts', the media, and ardent special interest groups into thinking otherwise. I maintain however that such notions that they teach are false and destructive to children's minds.

When teachers teach innocent children about sexual matters they can easily fall into the realm of teaching them to 'tolerate' immorality, whether on purpose or not. These teachers are relative thinkers at best and ignorant, unprincipled thinkers at worst. The amazing things is that the many parents of these children, are too trusting and not aware about the precariousness of public education that gives teachers permission to 'preach' their secular religion to innocent children.

The bible refers to pornographers as 'purveyors of filth'. Can this description cross over into the realm of education in the form of 'sex-education'? I think that it can, and especially when the adults who establish the sex education curriculum are without morals themselves and can even be titillated by the whole bizarre and destructive process that they are given power over by myopic administrators.

Some people regard family relationships as ultimate relationships. Not me. There is something that is more important than 'blood lines' and that is what I call 'spirit lines'. Spirit lasts forever. When you die you will be embalmed. Your blood will be drained and then washed down the sewer.

Spirit, however, will last forever. Blood lines will not. Spiritual bonds are the ultimate bonds. As Jesus said when he was told His family was waiting to see Him when He was 'on tour':

> *"whosoever shall do the will of my Father which is in heaven,*
> *the same is my brother, and sister and mother."*
>
> *– Matthew 12:50*

BOB'S OBBS (observations on children's education)

Parenting is a life long commitment, but 'intense' parenting should not be life long. There comes a time when parents need to let go or it might become similar to being in prison when adversarial forces enter in.

It is sometimes difficult to raise happy children outside of a good community that has moral standards. Because immorality is flourishing in this twenty first century, some people will desire another kind of community. I speak of a faith-based community, such as one that is built on religious faith, charity and good common sense values. I do believe that such a system is <u>essential</u> for stability and long-term happiness.

It is important that children and parents like each other's company. A good way to make sure that there is a certain amount of laughter in the house. I think that making children laugh is more important than buying them expensive toys. Any counseling that the parents have to offer on moral principles is a good thing, and it will show the children that their parents genuinely care about the children having good influences. Such will be totally useless to a child however, if those parents themselves are untrue to those principles that they teach.

Most children go to a public school as they grow up. This is, like it or not, a socializing process orchestrated by the powers that be in the educational system, none of whom are perfect human beings. Kids are always learning, and in school, they learn from their teachers and from their peers. If a particular teacher, or curriculum, is boring or irrelevant to the child and they think it is a waste of time, what does the child learn from the fact if they are forced to study it in depth? They experience 'negative learning' in such cases. By that, I mean that they learn that society, and their parents, seem to have given the 'okay' to the fact that wasting time can be a good thing. Thus, not all 'school' learning is good or productive, and a parent should be aware at all times what is going on when the larger society has a hand in the development of children.

Teaching children about the most important things in life should take place in the home first; not in the schools and not on the street or the playground; in the home.

God is eternal. Families, unless they are linked with God, are not eternal. If a parent wants their family to be an eternal family, in spirit at least, it only makes sense that <u>spiritual links</u> needs to be sought out.

Those would be links with higher spiritual powers and higher knowledge and stable beliefs about how people should treat each other.

Regarding our families, the words of the apostle John are very revealing in defining what happiness is:

> *"I have no greater joy than to hear that my children walk in truth."*
>
> *– 3 John 1: 4*

It has been said that, for a child's sake, the most important thing a parent can do is to love their spouse. Even divorced parents should treat each other with respect, if only for the children's sake. However you look at it, it is never good for a child to know that the two people who created them cannot stand to live with each other. Civility should always rule when the tragedy of a family breakup occurs. A child should never get the idea that he, or she, is the result of an 'unrighteous union'.

I would hesitate to judge any family, but I do have a question about close families whose members have lots of family pride, but no strong spiritual or sacred beliefs. My question is: if a family has no mutually held faith and their family ship eventually sinks, in a spiritual sense, will they, when they are together at the bottom of the ocean, will they find solace in the fact that they are all still together and still love one another, or will they resent each other because they <u>enabled</u> each other to fail in their most important purpose in life?

> *"I would say that the best thing a parent or teacher can do for a child is to help to instill in them a love for life and a love for learning."*
>
> *– Reverend Bob (from the book 'Life Goes On')*

The main goal in my life is to develop a personal character that is, or will be, in sync with that of heavenly beings, ones who I desire to share a heavenly abode with in eternity. I also wish the same for my posterity. Thus, I need to somehow find, or to <u>create,</u> a spirit of satisfaction. (*Do I hear Keith Richard's guitar playing?*) with occasional moments of bliss. This should take place in my house and with the spouse who I have chosen to share my life with.

There may be things about everybody that we do not like, but there are things about everybody that we <u>do</u> like, or even adore. In a marriage, if we focus on the things we do like about people, we will probably have a happy family. That is, as long as the people involved have a way of staying humble, respectful and find value in all of the members exercising the process of self-improvement.

You do not need to <u>be</u> all things to your children. It is more important just to <u>be there</u>.

An important aspect of raising children is finding a balance between protecting them, which includes invoking discipline, and empowering them, which includes allowing them to take certain risks.

Sometimes children resent parents because they see them as not knowing how to have any fun. Sometimes, the children may be right in that assessment.

We show our children that we love them by providing for their needs, by showing affection for them and by raising them in an environment of faith. This is so that they can see, by our words, deeds and our general attitude, that life has a definite purpose.

It would be my greatest personal accomplishment if my children grew up to be happy and honorable people with the ability and confidence to create their own honorable destinies. Let us face facts, this usually does not happen without having good guidance of some kind.

It would cause a parent much heartache to watch their children fall into a lifestyle that was wayward, fruitless, filthy or addictive. This would be even more tragic if the parents themselves were to fall into such a lifestyle. Yet there are billions of dollars spent today for just that purpose of luring young people into acquiring degenerate habits and attitudes like drunkenness, taking drugs, deadly or not, and seeking recreational sex. With so much money at work to persuade young people to the minimum results, let us never make the mistake of thinking that our children will be immune to such persuasions.

Parents, be a light to your children, not a dark mystery.

Peers can be of great influence to children. It is good for parents to know the children who your children associate with in the community, and to also know the parents of those peers as well.

It is not a matter of intolerance or snobbery, but I have come to the conclusion that if you let your child associate with other children who have no morals, you can wipe out years of hard work and good breeding in just a few weeks.

My goal as a parent is to provide for the needs of my family and create the best emotional climate possible for my children to grow up in. That might, or might not, be difficult, but it is definitely a full time job.

I think that it is a parent's duty to teach their children three basic things by word and deed. One; that they are loved; two; that life is basically good, and three; that there are many harmful habits and traps that people can fall into.

I suspect that a certain amount of tension is necessary in any family, even healthy families. It is good for parents to try to channel tension in healthy ways with understanding and empathy and to temper it with goodwill and humor in order to prevent serious issues from becoming contentious.

The main thing we need to teach children when they are young is how to raise their own children when they get older. We teach this by example every moment of the day.

Teaching Christian principles in the home and having them attend church with you is no guarantee that your children will not rebel or be disrespectful, but I do believe that it will greatly cut down the odds of that happening.

Giving birth to a child and living with them in the same abode may be enough to be able to call yourself a parent, but not enough to call yourself a 'good' parent. That title needs to be earned.

Every woman I know has the potential to be a good wife and mother or a bad one. Every man I know has the potential to be a good husband and father or not. It is the duty of everyone to encourage those of the same and opposite sex to fulfill their roles with integrity for the sake of themselves, their children, and my children, and for all of society, as well as for future generations. It is that important.

A parent has a duty to look out for their children's welfare and to let them know that they are loved. When parents get old, the children might have the same duty towards the parents. Nevertheless, that is about the extent of our obligations and, in the end, I think that we will all desire to spend our time (and even eternity) with those people who we genuinely care about and those people who genuinely care about us.

Should a parent abandon their child because he or she is stubborn or rebellious? No. Should a parent support their child in his, or her, stubbornness or rebelliousness? No. What to do then? Parents must wait until certain moments when the child is able and willing to be accepting of good teachings and good spiritual thoughts and feelings, and then use gentle powers of persuasion at that moment to convince them to 'choose the right'. Timing and planning are important. You can let a child go without abandoning them as the Bible talks about in the parable of the prodigal son. (Luke 15: 11-32)

The best way to teach children, or anyone else, is by example. Do the right things in all situations and the ones who love you will be influenced to do things your way. This is not autocratic or manipulative. It is simply your duty as a good parent.

A child's opinions should never be ignored. They should always be listened to and to be asked politely what their rationale is. Do not be afraid to talk about sensitive subjects, but at the right place and the right time. A family council can provide such a place and time for those discussions. If people refuse to accept reasonable views, then certain topics can become hot-button issues and then family members might tend to avoid all discussions, which never solves anything.

It is always great to be a part of a close and growing family. In closing, let me say that think that welcoming a new baby into the family and into the world can be the greatest feeling that any family` can have.

CHAPTER 14

Shake It Off

Monday Dec 13, 2021

This morning I remembered a sin I committed when I was a young teenager. It wasn't extremely serious, but even years after it happened, I was filled with a stifling regret about it. So that day I got out of bed and I began to write down some thoughts.

When I recall a bad memory from the past, it can cause me to feel depressed. It tends to haunt me because that memory seems to be frozen in time and it can cause my spirit to shrink. Thus, I want to just mentally escape from the world when that happens, either by fantasizing about something else that is more pleasing or by just going back to bed and ignoring any promptings to go forward with faith.

I will add that it t can be difficult for a person to go forward with faith in a world where that person has little, or no, faith in. There was not too many options for me to consider at the time I am talking about,, but I decided in the end, to simply just shake it off. How does a person do that one might ask. As it happens, I am of the opinion that, given my preoccupation with spiritual things, I think that I am fairly qualified to answer the call to do that.

I decided that that was the answer I needed. I've got to SHAKE IT OFF.

I took my own decision to heart but I knew that there were some preparatory thoughts that I needed to reflect on first. I said a little prayer about how grateful I was to have a number of good things happen to me in recent years. Then I began to think back. I thought about the day when I got baptized about thirty years ago. I remembered the day when I first received, by God's grace, the tools I would need to 'shake off' any bad influences that would enter into my mind.

Near the beginning of May 1990, I had a definite spiritual prompting that I should accept the offer to get baptized in the church of Jesus Christ of Latter Day Saints. I found the doctrine in that church very sensible and words of the early prophets in the church were also sensible. They taught, among other things, about the divinity of Jesus Christ and about the righteous principles of faith, hope and charity.

I also felt a good spirit there when I went to sacrament services in one of their chapels or when I fellowshipped with the members. I was baptized after about a year and a half of studying the Scriptures. That included the Bible and the Book of Mormon. Although I did not realize it fully at the time, but that spiritual decision turned out to be exactly what I needed at that time in my life.

I remembered the night after my baptism as I was falling asleep in my bed at home. At one point, just before I was about to fall asleep, I thought that I perceived another presence in my bedroom. For some unknown reason, I thought that it was not a good presence. I thought it might be some kind of evil spirit, or even a demon who liked to stalk people from a distance. I felt him coming closer to me on my bed, so I tried to turn around but I could not. It was like I was paralyzed. Anyways, I could move my arm so I quickly raised my fist in the air. It was not something I thought out in advance, it was more like an automatic reaction. I thought that it would take him by surprise if I showed him, or she, or it that I was quite aware of what was going on.

I tried to turn around and face him, but for some reason I could not turn around. It was like I was paralyzed. In any case, my mind was active so I was able to come out of my sleep state and that stopped that evil spirit, or whatever it was, from coming any further into my personal space. I could sense that it was retreating after I raised my fist in the air to show him/her/it that I was awake and fully aware of what was going on.

At that moment and I perceived that the demon became aware that I would not tolerate him coming into my presence and that I was prepared to fight against him. I think that raising my fist in the air took him by surprise and sent him a warning message that I was once again in my conscious mind and I was aware of his presence. Because I was now aware of him, we both knew that his disguises would be of no use to him. Demons, like their master know how to use disguises well. One of the main disguises they use is that of a harmless or innocuous entity, the kind of entity or person who I would ordinarily just ignore. Such a personality is only used to dull the senses of the spiritual predator.

In any case, that demon knew that I was no longer asleep or comatose. He knew that I would no longer acquiesce to my desired state of slumber and that I would fight against the presence of he/she/it and 'shake it off'.

Thus, I was able to shake off that 'thing' and caused him to flee from my presence. When I resisted his evil spell and fought back I regained an even fuller awareness that spirits need not be feared because they can only do damage when we allow the into our presence and when we do not give consent to their wishes.

After that experience, I felt a peace come into my room. Thus, I regained my composure and the knowledge that I had in the back of my mind that I still had a good purpose in life. Soon I became fully awake in my bed and I thought about that experience. Most importantly, I knew that I was now in a much safer place than I was before.

My baptism really was a wonderful event, even though I wasn't smart enough at the time to know about all of the implications it would have, I do remember that on that day there were many prayers were said for me by the righteous people who were present there in the chapel that day. That gave me some comfort.

That experience of 'SHAKING IT OFF' was a large part of the solution I needed for my mental stability. It was a solution that was given to me as a gift from a higher power and it allowed my mind to be set free. It was certainly not my idea that such a good thing as that would happen to me. I had also received a spiritual prompting a few days earlier that baptism was the correct path for me. I did not personally know what would happen after I stepped into the water, but for some time I suspected that there was something going on in that church that I was investigating and I wanted to know what it was.

It became clear to me then that I only needed to accept the gift of spiritual courage that that God bestowed upon me at that time. I also wanted to see if it was possible that my spirit could be reclaimed both by my Heavenly Father and by my higher self. It was a great relief for me, when, after that day, I began to feel that I was indeed reclaimed and that I would henceforth and often have spiritual truths come into my mind from an unknown source.

'I will shake off all bad influences', I said to myself. When I realized that I had the power to do that, I knew that I would be assisted by the Spirit of the Holy Ghost whose purpose was to testify to us of the divinity of Jesus Christ. That was an uplifting feeling and was accompanied by feelings of trust.

I decided that I would discard the mental state of being lulled into carnal thinking by a demon that happened to be watching me and who was hoping that I would slip back into that impotent state of mind numbing sleep. I decided that I would not allow that to happen. Thus, I figured that the 'thing' would then be banished from my presence, at least temporarily. I felt that I would then, once again, breathe in the fresh air of freedom and that would cause my soul to become literally **refreshed.**

Sometimes, when I have bad thoughts, I can escape by going on to face book and catching up on world opinions, especially the good opinions that are there. There are a limited amount of good opinions there, but I always have the opportunity to use my discernment and use the good thoughts for my personal motivation. Sometimes, though, the good opinions that I seek are not there and I miss them.

Fortunately, I subscribe to a few reliable face book groups, run by Christians, who see it as their sole purpose to inspire other people with wise words from a wise man or wise woman or a motivating passage from the scriptures. Many times those wise words have proven to inspire me and send me on my way with a nugget of a comforting truth that is there for me to hold on to.

The internet can be dangerous, but less dangerous than relying on the hormones in my brain that help me to recall the wickedness I have seen in the past and the foolishness within the wicked realms that I once allowed myself to partake of. The gospel warns me that contemplating those realms would cause me to be unworthy of entering into my Heavenly Father's presence. Thus, I knew that I would need to abandon those harmful realms, even deadly realms, at all cost.

I am grateful that this knowledge of the power of making my own choice was delivered to me by the grace of my God on that night. As well, I will now try more often to recall that time after my baptism when I put that demon bully in his place and caused him to literally 'run away'. The fact remains that on that night I had been redeemed by God's grace and to deny that would be to refuse to accept my redemption. I swear at this time that I will never do that.

THE FOUNDATION

I was thinking about some problems I was having in my life and I thought about my personal antidote that I have used in the past to overcome problems in general. I am referring here to my personal testimony of Jesus Christ, or the Messiah. It is of ultimate importance because it is the only name by which people like me can preserved in a state of peace, freedom and in some cases, joy.

I was thinking about 'the cognitive abyss' that I fell into many years ago. It happened in April,1990, thirty years ago when I was a single parent and living in Winnipeg. It was the night before I was to be baptized at my church. I went to bed and I was monitoring my thoughts. I said a prayer before bed and I felt at some point during in my sleep that I was falling into an abyss, a dark hole of some sort. There seemed to be no end to that hole or to my fall. It was very disturbing and I felt a sense of hopelessness.

The night <u>after</u> my baptism, on May the nineteenth 1990, I said a prayer again, and I went to bed. I dreamed again that I was falling into that same dark hole, but this time it was different. After falling for some time, I felt that I hit something.

It was not a hard thing that I hit, but it was solid and it stopped my fall. It was a foundation of some kind. It may have been rocks or it may have been fertile soil, or maybe both. I don't know, but <u>it was just there</u> in that panacea of my mind and it stopped my fall immediately.

I knew I had landed on something and whatever it was it was something that was not there the night before. I only knew that it was a sign of something good. I could not explain what it was or even what it felt like. I just knew there was something there. That 'ground' also had a sign of life in it, or at least, an ability to preserve life. In any case I was not a man without hope any longer. The perceived 'pit' that I fell into now had a bottom of some kind, a bottom where I could once again feel a certain stability and even 'feel life'.

Fast forward to this morning 9.00 A.M. Nov. 28. 2021. I was thinking about my testimony and my witness of the Spirit. I knew that my testimony was still there and had been there for the last thirty years.

I got out of bed, but I didn't feel very good. My body ached. So I went back to sleep. I woke up about an hour and a half later and I felt 100% better. It might have been that I was aware of my foundation again, but this time it was different than thirty years earlier. I was feeling bliss lines. It was a great feeling. My earlier feelings of discomfort had disappeared. I was feeling refreshed.

I think it was because the vision I had on the night of my baptism came back into my mind and a remnant of the message that I received was still there. I figured that thirty years of gospel study entitled me to feel that feeling still. In any case, my spiritual foundation had returned to me and returned in a in a better form than ever.

How did it do that? I didn't really do anything to instigate a foreign presence in my house, but something was happening to me, and in a good way. I was being acted upon, but in a good way. I could not explain it perfectly, but you would need to read my past journal entries over the years to catch on to how I was feeling and what knowledge I had been able to gather over the years and after many visits to the Holy Temple.

I felt like I had my testimony renewed. I thought about my brother David and was worried about him after hearing from another friend that his cancer tests were not successful. 'He needed to hear about the 'Foundation', I thought. He also needs to hear about the importance of baptism, even baptism for the dead, by those in authority.

My brother and I were similar kinds of people as some brothers are. Despite our differing political opinions we were still fairly close to each other. He, as opposed to myself, was not interested in studying matters from a religious or a theological viewpoint.

I wanted to tell him about the things that I had learned over time, but it was not easy because for one thing, he lived twelve hundred miles from me and for another thing, it is not always easy to challenge another person's tightly held belief system, whether it was based upon a God or based upon some kind of secular/humanist philosophy. Most people can be very adamant about maintaining a belief system that they have held for literally decades.

I felt that I had had many revelations or epiphanies over the years, but they were not the cataclysmic type of revelation where there was a rapture that happened. It was more like a slow and steady progress. It was 'line upon line, precept upon precept, here a little and there a little' *(Isaiah 28: 10)*. This is an idea that I learned from the book of Isaiah in the Old Testament.

These learning experiences were compounded over the years and led me to possess a secure testimony of spiritual things. A testimony like that could only come by the evidence of spiritual things being presented to me by a mysterious outside power. That is exactly the way it happened. Not only that, it could happen to anybody if they put forward the effort to learn about those things.

Even if the unlearned souls manage to learn a few true principles, it can still be an uncertain learning environment because there are still a lot if unexpected factors in the big picture. As a philosopher once said, "a little bit of knowledge is a dangerous thing". Life, as well as relationships can be very complicated and exactness is not an option in the celestial kingdom of God. Exactness will be a necessity.

Hence, I have come to the decision to have my brother to be vicariously baptized in the nearest Holy temple. There are over one hundred temples on the earth and the people who are assigned to work in those temples have been ordained by worthy souls to do specific jobs there. Those jobs will need to be done for the sake of the freshly baptized souls who gather there and who will be overjoyed to hear their names mentioned as candidates for placement on the 'rolls of the faithful'. Those are the ones and who will be added to the list of the many who will receive vicarious baptisms and confirmations.

Not only that, but we are promised in the church that those souls who need enlightenment and intelligence will get it, assuming that they are sincere and humble and willing to pay the price of righteous loyalty towards those who have sacrificed much for us.

In other words, I could say that <u>the angels will literally, teach those souls</u>. Such will be a great learning experience for them, one that will be comparable to none other. Furthermore those souls will rejoice when they hear the things that are taught to them because they will know that those things are a necessary passwords into the realms of Eternal life.

I can only hope that the false learning experiences that certain people had in this mortal world will not be embedded in their characters. If they are 'embedded' then those souls may then be classed by the holiest of standards, as incorrigible. But I do not feel too sorry for them because, for the most part, it might be that they will be getting exactly what they want.

I say this because it is my belief that the hardest thing for people to do in this life is to get rid of bad habits and cynical attitudes that have become embedded into their characters. Thus, it will take nothing less than their own sincere repentance, and as well a compassionate act of God to bring a lasting healing to them.

It might also be noted that the stable saints, those being the ones who have chosen the right path will be granted a foundation underneath their feet so that they can gain traction and stability whenever they move and act. It is much easier for a person to 'shake something off' if they are standing on solid ground. Otherwise, they will just be 'twisting in the wind'. I pray that the honest souls among them will be able to plant their feet firmly on the ground if and when they accept the wonderful invitation to move forward to a better and a more enlightened place.

As for me, I know not what the future holds. I do not know where I will end up. I do know of a surety though that I have been given a spiritual firmament underneath my feet from which I can speak the truth and stand strong. I have also been given the tools I need to be able to get to a special place that was given to me for the express purpose of making me happy. Those are the most important things there are in this world.

C H A P T E R 15

Bob's Obbs #1 Random observations from Bhs (Bob's higher self)

BOB KING QUOTES The personal quotes in this chapter are mostly from the Daily Ahem, a blog by Bob King, a.k.a. Reverend Bob, a.k.a. Dr. Elias Ibblestrom

It is in my deepest private moments of peace when I ask my Heavenly Father to assist me in my healing and in the healing of those around me. This is so that I will remember the intensity of my covenants with Him and I will be reminded of my sincere love for Him.

There are only two kinds of writing. The first is writings that cause a person's soul to shrink by describing depressing scenes or describing depression in general. The second kind is writings that uplift a person's soul by describing how we can escape all that and find deliverance from depressing scenes and depression in general.

The simple power of prayer: There is a haunted house somewhere in the consciousness or subconscious mind of every person. They are ugly things there that are maintained by evil entities to torment all children of God. It is intimidating because it is a very chaotic realm and it is intimidating also because of its sheer ugliness. Don't ever go there. If you should stumble into that place accidentally, ask God to make it vanish. He has the power to do that. As well, <u>He has the love to do it for you upon your request.</u>

Regarding the prospect of a nuclear war; a fervent plea by an innocent impassioned sixteen year old is just as meaningful as the protests of an experienced fifty year old nuclear scientist because the young person has just as much to lose as the older scientist, maybe even more to lose. Nevertheless, the idea of avoiding war at any cost is not totally valid. That is because some things can be worth dying for, like living in a state of freedom instead of living in a state of being enslaved by an evil conqueror.

I dreamed I was playing chess with someone. I thought about the nature of the game and I thought about my opponent's strategy. But when I thought about my own strategy I knew that that was the most important of all strategies. On further consideration, I suspect that this dream was not really about chess.

It will be Mingle with angels. An angel might be a spiritual being or he, or she, might be a real person. If they are truly good a real person will be of the same mentality as an angel. Mingle with those angelic people whenever you can. If you had a precious friend or relative who is now deceased, remember them and the good things they stood for, as often as you can. They will appreciate it. And your association according to the good memories you had when they were living are invaluable things.

The powers of darkness will always declare that they have the authority to judge the powers of light. That is why they are called the powers of <u>darkness</u>, because it is the best environment in which to deceive. The darkness that surrounds untruth can help to make false authority look like true authority.

Yes, bad things happen to good people, but when those bad things are properly dealt with, the good people become even better people.

It can be a good thing when we <u>detach</u> from people and things that are not good for us. If we have become comfortable with those people or things, it will probably be necessary for us to <u>attach</u> to something else to fill that void after we detach from the other people and things. Be wise as you search for that substitute so that you do not make the same kind of mistake.

<u>Stay ahead</u> of your enemies, enablers and agitators. You've got to detach from them to make that happen. The space between them and you will be based upon one who is more righteous. This higher state must be accomplished with humility and without boasting, but if you don't <u>detach</u> from them they will <u>attach</u> to you and you will end up using all your energy to haul them around behind you.

Without the light of Christ in our lives our joys are all illusions. Thus, we are all beggars. We can have no real joy and no true love without Him. In the end we will lack the physical and spiritual necessities of life. We will have nothing but darkness and dirtiness and the vague memory of what was a potentially joyful experience.

Some people are so envious and bitter that they will try to spread their bitterness over to those who they envy and try to cause them to become permanently bitter like themselves. For you to take seriously the accusations of those envious people is just what they want and that would be a serious mistake on your part to indulge in that.

I know that peer pressure has always had a strong influence in young people's lives. I have no proof, but I strongly suspect that social media has made <u>peer pressure</u> much more present than it was in the past. On the positive side, that means that we will have more opportunities to stand up for the right. That is, in a way, a good thing because It gives us a chance to shine. It is good to shine, whether others see our light or not.

"Remember the Sabbath Day and keep it holy. The Sabbath Day approaches. Let us go to a GOOD place on that day. It should be a place where a <u>GOOD</u> spirit abides. We will share that <u>GOOD</u> spirit with people who we regard as <u>GOOD</u> friends. Does that sound like a <u>GOOD</u> plan?"

"If you are certain of your knowledge, use it like a bird uses its wings. Let knowledge set you free instead of weighing you down. If you feel you have knowledge, but yet you cannot get off the ground and fly freely, it is probably because you are 'hanging around' with turkeys instead of eagles."

Today I will take the next step upwards in my daily contemplative journey. It may be only a slightly higher step, but in eternity, that small 'upwards' step is a giant step. Eternal things have a different scale. That is because eternity contains a certain amount of light that will separate us from the darkness."

Some people think that it is only heaven or hell that await us after death. I don't believe that, but I believe there is a heaven and that it is a place with many staggered levels where some levels are higher than others. This is made clear in 1ˢᵗ Corinthians 15: 40 – 42.

By the way, the word 'unconditional', as pertaining to 'unconditional love', is not found in any scriptures.

The leading cause of premature death in western society is not cancer or heart attacks or suicide or accidents, etc. It is the inability for people to change their physical and mental habits that eventually lead to the above-mentioned things.

It is a wonderful thing to be able to change something that was considered second rate into something that is first rate. Nevertheless, it is better all around to settle for second best in reality than accept first best in a fantasy.

The Christian philosopher Soren Kierkegaard is known for saying that religious conversion always requires a 'leap of faith'. I say that may be partially true, but I say that after one gains spiritual knowledge, and only then, does the leap forward become a shorter, easier and safer leap than the leap backwards into doubt and resentment.

Despite the many things that torment me these days, I still have my moments of bliss. I still have breath in my body. I still have the knowledge that God loves me. I am doing all right. Do I have enemies? Yes, and if you are a decent person who loves liberty, you will have enemies too. I guarantee it. Nevertheless, with my God's help, my enemies will not defeat me.

"Go", said the brain. Nothing happened. "Go", said the body. Nothing happened. "Go", said the Spirit. Nothing happened. Unfortunately, they were all out of fuel. They all forgot to fill their tanks the night before. Thankfully, the Spirit had been built with a reserve tank in the back. It had enough fuel in it to drive itself and the other two vehicles to the nearest prayer station where they were all able to fill up. Everything went well after that."

"Can I receive a revelation or a prompting from God even if I do not deserve it? Yes, but I can receive it only if I have chosen to seek out His Word on a regular basis and if you choose to stand in Holy places. God always appreciates that and rewards it.

There is a difference between 'harder' and 'stronger'. A denial of the truth can make me hard of heart, but an affirmation of the truth, with its softness, can make me 'stronger' in heart. That is because truth will have a very definite presence there. Truth is a very tender thing and tenderness is a powerful resource even though it is a soft thing. Soft things can facilitate things that are very strong. 'Hardness' may be tough, but it is not humble and it is not much fun. Strength has a certain amount of softness and that actually can make it enjoyable to fight for things that are worth fighting for.

There are good people in all churches, Christian or not. There are also hypocrites in all churches, Christian or not. Thus, it is a matter of the abundance of good. The question is, 'which church has the most intelligence in their doctrine, and the most kindness in their members and in the most inspiring spiritual promptings that a person might experience when attending that church?' If that is true, then religious traditions alone are not always very relevant. People's goodness must be physically visible to be properly witnessed.

Many people will balk at the mention of the mere name of Jesus Christ. That is they're choice. If they will refuse to acknowledge Him or even talk about Him, they may do that for any number of reasons. but when people balk at the mere mention of His name, or balk at certain words like 'repentance' or 'faith', they unknowingly reveal something about themselves. And that 'something' is not good.

Sometimes we must draw moral 'lines in the sand' and not allow ourselves, or others, to cross those lines. Sometimes it can be tempting for people to ignore those lines and cross them or allow them to be crossed. The more righteous people among us are also the strongest and they will not back down. They will have the courage to speak the truth no matter what.

The time I have left in my life is like the money I have. I don't have much of either. Therefore, I should put much thought into thinking about the best ways to spend them both.

Regarding evil: The devil is real and like an expert fisherman, he knows what lures to use. Also, he does not play 'catch and release'. Once he gets his grasp on you he will proceed to squeeze every bit of pain and trouble out of you that he can, right up until the day you die. The only solution to that is to trust in God and fill your days with righteous endeavors."

I think that the ultimate question that awaits us all after this life might be – "Aside from trying to impose your own prideful opinions upon others about how they should live their lives, what have you done to make the world the place that you think it should be?

When I was young, I assumed that civics and even civility would never be displaced in this society. How wrong I was. Nowadays disrespect, narcissism, and people who believe in their own moral superiority are very common.

Have you and your spouse agreed on something recently that benefits you both and makes you feel good? Good. When those moments happen, appreciate them. Even if it's a small thing acknowledge it, then give your spouse a big smile and a HIGH FIVE.

We cannot find a higher realm of existence if we never choose to look in a higher direction. Heaven is right in front of us, but Hell is right in front of us too. Neither of these realms are visible. Heaven is hidden by the harsh reality of this world and Hell is hidden by it's own disguises.

There are two kinds of evil. One is stupid/evil and the other is evil/evil. When left without care or correction, the former will follow a natural path downwards and evolve into the latter.

Some ignorant people may be well intentioned, but they are still ignorant people, so don't be too trusting.

There are some people whose integrity I trust, but not their intelligence. Nevertheless, I try to be kind because God works with all of us in our own spheres and in His own time.

One of my favorite quotes from Peter 2:19 - "While they promise themselves liberty, they themselves are the servants of corruption: for of whom a man is overcome, of the same is he brought in bondage."

As we get older I feel it is incumbent on all of us, and for the sake of future generations to be able to declare near the end of it all what the main purpose of it is for people in general. In a sentence or two, what is your purpose? If you are <u>not</u> able to give a good answer to that question, does that not mean that you have literally <u>failed</u> in fulfilling your mission here on earth, that being to gain knowledge and keep it?

Artists and musicians - If you have been blessed with talent you will probably receive a certain amount of notoriety. If you do not use that notoriety well, you might do something stupid like proclaim your moral superiority to the world. That will not end well. Ego-driven habits are always born out of pride and perpetrated by selfishness. This is as opposed to being grateful for the creative gifts that you have been given.

I know there are some comparatively good people in the world who do not go to church. Perhaps they don't need to go to church and partake of the sacrament every week, I don't know. I only know that <u>I</u> do need to go. It is not a weakness. It is a physical medicine for me. It is an intelligent and effective antidote (99% of the time) that can bring healing.

The Holy Spirit is like a radio wave with a delicate frequency. I have a hard time tuning it in when my radio receptor (my capacitor) is either stuck or else over greased.

There are only two kinds of people in the world. They are those who need Jesus Christ and know it, and those who need Jesus Christ and don't know it.

Spiritual people are usually called to live their lives at an accelerated pace, but that will also include some calmer and slower things like caution and patience. It is also good to seek out, and fellowship, with others who have been called to work at that same pace. In some cases, it is a relay race, and you will need at some time to pass along the baton to another person.

Forgiveness is a process where self-cleansing can take place. Forgiveness will always make my life easier, because evil spirits will not be effective when they try to 'stir things up'. They will withdraw because they do not know how to fight against the 'forgiveness strategy'.

It is true that Jesus can wash away our sins, but the question is: 'what will be left over after the bath?

Statistics show that life is always more enjoyable for people who have a spiritual side to them and who know how to access that spiritual side. They are just happier people. If you have that opportunity to gain access to that spiritual side, use it regularly and do not let the pagans of the world take it away from you, even if your beliefs are not yet fully developed.

On inspiration: When making decisions we should think things out as much as we can and then make our decision based upon correct principles and reasoning, and then seek the Holy Ghost, who I sometimes call the great under-liner, or the great highlighter, to confirm the correctness of those decisions.

There is much evil in the world. Aside from having a connection to the Powers of heaven, the best way to fight it is through STRONG families. 'Strong' is the operative word here. Weak families, feeble-minded families, divided families, and even families who are fierce but lack understanding, will be of no use to anyone.

Having a strong family means having a collective wisdom, love, and the courage to protect each other. Families also need a spirit of gratitude, and a set structure for learning. Good spirits will attend you when your family commits to those things.

If you are not familiar with creative writing and using words well, I would highly recommend that you spend some time working at it. Keep a journal and I guarantee that will work to your advantage and to your children's advantage too. Once you have harnessed your words, then you can work on harnessing your imagination and your actions".

Just like there are stages in sleep, there are stages in wakefulness. Paradoxically, human beings do not usually recognize this. That is because they cannot recognize the lower and higher stages of wakefulness. Why not? It is because they are not 'awake' enough to do so.

When we connect with good things, that creates a bond that is invaluable. That bond, however, can be broken under pressure. The pressure may be a result of outside forces or inside forces, but nevertheless, the bond will always broken with our consent.

Some people may be well intentioned, but may be too naive to see where real evil lurks. Such well-intentioned people can do more damage than good when they try to save the world.

Observe a beautiful sunset. The elements of that sunset might be randomly placed in the atmosphere, but for those elements to even exist together in the first place, and in such a way that provides such reoccurring beauty, must surely be a sign of a great Creator and a true artist.

For God to have newness, it is required that that newness be aligned somehow with His nature, otherwise it would be foreign to him. <u>We human beings</u>, in our present state, are that newness. At the same time, we are not new or foreign to Him because we are His children.

I fully believe that God speaks to us today. The heavens are not closed. He would not abandon us in these most confusing of times. We just need to activate our spiritual radio and tune in to the right channel.

If sensible religion is of great importance, as I believe it is, then we can bet that <u>all</u> efforts will be made by evil forces to pervert it and discredit it. Given the fallen state of mankind, these efforts will often be successful. God and His prophets, however, <u>by the power of the priesthood</u>, still have the power to sanctify the true church.

The foundation of my faith is the covenants that I make in the Holy Temple, and also if I am able to live up to those covenants. If I can do that, then that is all I need to do. Simple. My job is done. My purpose is completed. I will be as permanently refreshed as I can possibly be and I thank my God in Heaven for that opportunity.

CHAPTER 16

The Power of Choice

Today I will choose to do what I want to do. It is my right to do so. Thus, I will do one of two things: I will - GO BACK TO SLEEP AND LET MY MIND FADE INTO OBLIVION **OR** I WILL GET UP AND DO SOMETHING GOOD. It is my choice.

The power of choice is one of our greatest blessings, Every thing is dependent on it, whether it led to be happiness or misery. The greatest thing about it is that, once in a while we are actually free to rescind our first choice and choose again. We are free to actually change our minds if we find that necessary.

Politically, I think it is difficult to live under a government that does not recognize the right of its citizens to have their freedom of choice. We usually have a constitution of some kind and/or a charter of rights to make sure that self appointed bureaucrats and police and even 'medi-crats' do not set up their own sets of laws that everyone should be expected to obey without question. In certain countries insurrections and revolutions have happened in order to prevent that from happening. Can it happen here? Anything is possible, but the arrogance of certain leaders is enough to make a rebellion a viable option.

How a country that I always thought was civilized could elect sim-pletons as leaders who believe that citizens should just obey orders and forget notions of free expression and stifle themselves hold no value in freedom of choice is beyond my comprehension.

I will be very frank here. When I look at a picture of a grinning old fool like Joe Biden in the in the USA or a smug 'little boy' like Justin Trudeau in Canada, I feel overcome by what can only be described as a feeling of <u>repulsion</u>. Nevertheless, I have faith that eventually a good change is going to come. There are just too many smart and brave people in the U. S. A. and Canada to let a good country get so blind.

The hostility that I feel is a feeling that I honestly try to keep harnessed. Nevertheless, I will try to rein in my hostility because I still have hope that people will, one day, decide to forsake their selfish interests for the sake of establishing both peace and rational thinking. I will admit though that I am often perplexed by it. Is that my fault. It doesn't matter because I see it as a trend and if it is a trend, it will probably become an established trend means and that probably means there will be no end to it.

I have come across false doctrines as I have travelled around the realms of the popular culture of our time and of our country. That was a culture that could be blatant or subtle or even ridiculous, but anytime that I paid attention to it, I found that it always managed to prevent my soul from advancing to higher realms. Something was just 'not right' about it.

It is one of my purposes in life to stick to that high standard of independent and rational merit-based thinking as well as maintaining a kinder attitude towards people on a personal level. I still have an expectation of people to be honest and fair-minded and at this point in my life.

Over the years, I have become smarter about things like trying to rebel just for the sake of rebelling much like the 'Antifa' movement does. I now see them as a destructive nuisance at best, even though I can usually do nothing about them as law enforcement people too often turns a blind eye to them. They just make life more frustrating, as if it is not frustrating enough already. They are realms of dependency that too many people tolerate and that some people even promote.

Unfortunately, those people do not know when they've been duped. Even so, such thinking is not acceptable to me, even though I was once caught up in it myself to some degree when I was a young and idealistic university student. It was like some wicked and distant being was telling me horror stories that I once found interesting, but after some time, they only brought out feelings of repulsion.

Hence, the only way I can escape that is to get back into bed and go to sleep. That solves the problem in an immediate sense, but it never actually solves problems permanently. The problems, in fact, just seem to get worse. That can create many whole new problems, especially when I associate with people who lack understanding.

That has created a hole in my life and it is a real thing. A hole is basically a circle, an empty circle that encompasses nothingness. Is such a hole a valid jumping off point into productive things? No. There is no traction to be found in an empty hole. It is a useless space. So how can I jump off into a productive space when any move I make produces nothing positive?

The only thing I can do is wait upon the Lord and wait for Him to fill my empty space with something of worth. I know that He has the power to do that. I also know that I cannot do that by myself. I have no traction. I have no solid ground beneath my feet. So I will have the faith that he will do it for me, as long as I am patient and worthy of it.

Yet, I now realize that I am a mature man (finally) and as I gather myself according to the kind of person who I have always wanted to become, I find myself resolving to be happy. I still have that opportunity and that alone makes me feel better about things.

Before You Think

Before you think about anything, ask yourself, will you try to be positive and constructive or will you try to be negative and critical? It doesn't matter if the country of your birth has gone crazy and has elected a selfish power hungry fool as leader, you still have a basic philosophical choice to make. There are always other things you can focus on.

The collective conscience of the left just might tell them someday that they will likely betray their own ideals if they let the citizens suffer because of their policies. That is, if the Tsunami of political correctness has not washed away all of their reasoning abilities. If they survive that Tsunami they just might just decide to reclaim their sanity. So I say that everybody should have faith in honest work and don't give up hope.

If people are somewhat aware that their lives really are going out of control, then they might just think about reestablishing strong rules that they should live by. Many megalomaniacal leaders of political movements will continue to push the sheep down the socialist dead end path, and most of the sheep will follow them, as has always been their tradition. They will play off each other with their constant rhetoric and they will proceed down onto the bottomless pit from which there is no return, especially the ones who have always received exorbitant salaries for the work they have done in the past as they try to extend their perceived virtue to the unwashed masses.

But the piper must be paid, and even though the establishment of good rules and self-disciplinary measures could be the very thing that people need, many people will proceed forward down the icy slope. It could be the same way for a person if they feel that someone else, or something else, is controlling their life. They might not come out and admit that to others, but their actions and personalities will probably somehow show it. That will be a definite sign that a 'change' in attitude needs to happen, if it is not already too late. Nevertheless, some people will ignore that suggestion and just go with what seems to be the easiest option and put their faith in something that is even more risky, like plain dumb luck.

Many people, out of a need for comfort and security, will confine themselves to a low personality default mode, and hope to just stay out of harm's way. Such people will be satisfied to live off other people's money, but that money will only last so long.

That may be justifiable in their own minds because they know, in their hearts, that they are basically lost souls in a lost world, but instead of trying to di something about their status, they might just anoint themselves as legitimate victims and look for the next government subsidy. Given the state if the world today, or society, the ground that they stand on is shaky at best, so 'why worry' they tell themselves, just be happy. Even though, if they are truthful they will admit that they aren't really happy at all.

That is because they can now actually perceive a wolf coming to their door and they know that they have not put forth the effort to prepare for, and consider, measures of austerity, or even discover the real world and the principles of personal effort that exist there.

No matter if you view life as drudgery or as a circus or as something beautiful, sometimes we just need guidance. I say that the more that we gain enough knowledge to embrace the good things on life and eliminate the bad things, and the more we appreciate hard work, then the more that people will find joy in their lives.

We all have a tendency to wallow in mediocrity and dither about important issues, but some people, even leaders of nations with an army at their fingertips, can neglect the value of personal initiative in their thoughts to the point where they underestimate, or totally ignore, their power to control the direction of their own thoughts, and therefore, lose the power to control their own lives and the lives of their citizens.

(IE: Pol pot in Cambodia, Mao Tze Tung in China and Joseph Stalin in Russia) *Are you noticing a pattern here?*

Thus, they come to lack the confidence in their ability to choose their own thoughts and will yield to some kind of extremism. They ignore what they should focus on and make the most of dreaming dreams of fantasy and denying reality. They do not yet realize that they are free to leap from one thought pattern to another. The best and most important leap they can make here is to leap from a negative thought spiral (downward) to a positive thought spiral (upward). That is not a cop-out or an escape mechanism. It the exercising of a God given gift to **change**, that everyone has been given.

It often seems evident that people who deny their right to choose to fully exercise the abilities that they have been blessed with are negligent people. Whether they do that because they are afraid or lazy or whether it is because they just choose to follow the crowd, they will, in the end, only be able to accomplish a minimum of success, and even more likely, perish with their prideful egos and their disappointing legacies in tow.

I am not just attacking people who don't see things my way. I have fallen into traps myself in the past and may do so in the future. Nevertheless, I have special sources of wisdom like inspirational books that provide me with unique and thought provoking perspectives. Everyone should have sources of wisdom like that. It is totally sensible that it is a noble ambition for everyone to have a desire to improve themselves. Everyone.

I will stand by those sources until I meet anyone can prove me wrong about them. Despite what some people might think, I welcome anyone who could give me a good philosophical debate or offer some good advice on establishing important life skills.

When I write about correct ways of thinking, I am not talking so much about intellectualism, but I am talking about fairness and sacrifice and trying to set up the best overall work environment, one that will help all of us and not feed the get-rich-quick mentality.

Resisting Temptation

Personally, I now know better than to succumb to cheap thrills and sensationalism, and I will not partake of untruth in any form. I will not go backwards when a clear and intelligent forward path beckons to me. I have been given many gifts in my life like revelations, guidance, faith, friends, etc. Those things have allowed me to progress and move forward in my chosen realm. I have progressed and I have allowed myself to learn new things. If a person does not recognize and appreciate their progression, then I am afraid that they have not really progressed at all.

One thing I know for sure, as ironic as it might seem, that is that it takes strength to admit your weaknesses. Another thing I know for sure is that it takes gratitude when you receive strength, physically and mentally. Because of that gratitude, you will then be able to make proper use of that strength and share it with others. God gives that to us freely so that, with a bit of effort on our part, we might overcome all of our weaknesses. He said that in the latter days He would pour His Spirit upon us.

> *"And it shall come to pass afterward that I will pour out my spirit on all flesh; your sons and your daughters shall prophesy, and your old men **shall** dream dreams."*
>
> *– Joel 2:28*

I will be loyal to Jesus Christ and trust in Him, so that He might help me in whatever righteous efforts I have and hope that He will deliver me, in the end, to a place where I might find peace. He said that He would do that for me, and even though I tried to do it on my own, I find now that I cannot. I am not strong enough or smart enough or determined enough.

Thankfully though, I do have a willing spirit and a sense of peace about life in general. Those two things are enough for me to either ignore my imperfections or do whatever I need to do to correct them and then advance. Thus, I will rely on His grace to redeem me and on his wisdom to help me make my pathways clear and on his strength to give me the courage I need. Thus, freedom, or liberty, and the maintaining of it, are prime concerns for me and should be for anyone who seeks a solid purpose in their life.

There was a time when I found it difficult to resist carnal thoughts and urges. It is not always easy to change the body's chemistry regarding compulsions, but sometimes it just needs to be done if we are to progress. It is basically a test. Whether we want to take the test or not, it doesn't matter. It is required of you for the reason that it is the only way that your progress can be measured. That is where divine rules come in. God bless any man or woman who is able to receive those rules and exercise them in the same spirit of love in which they were given.

Personally, I do not think that I would be worthy of Eternal life without a connection to Christ. That is the number one factor in my life. Thus, I must stand in Holy places as often as I can and with all of the distractions around me. That may not be always easy to do. Nevertheless, if we don't decide to do it, we will surely be without hope and that is a fact of life.

With my age and with my health problems, I must admit that I often feel half dead. But then, I also feel half alive. And the half of me that feels alive, often feels very much alive. Thus, I am resolved to recognizing those times, and by recognizing them, being able to summon them at my will when I need to call on them. By God's grace, they will come to me and with the accompanying Holy Spirit that comes with them.

I recently became aware that I have mentioned a certain principle in the books that I write that is, as far as I know, mostly coming from my own mind. It concerns **the higher self of human beings and the**

lower self of human beings. In short, the higher self is concerned with righteous and good principles. The lower self is concerned with lower principles, including unrighteous principles and carnal principles. There are no exceptions to this.

In an ideal world, or in the realm of Heaven itself, it would make that higher world a more ideal world, that is if the will of the human being, man or woman, were to allow it to be so. It then would follow that the higher self would, or should, rule over their lower self. This I declare is a basic fact of the human mind. It might even be THE basic fact of the human mind, and maybe even the animal mind as well.

I will say right now that I do not have a PhD in psychology, but that doesn't matter to me. I have taken some courses and I find most of the psychological subjects that I studied so far ism.to be faulty at best. I have also been studying psychology privately, or 'on my own', for a long time.

This is why I say that this theory of mine about the dual nature of the human mind is a 'truism'. Not only do I see it as a true theory, but I see it as a <u>fact</u> and I believe it to be true with EVERY FIBRE OF MY BEING. I will add that many of the psychological principles that I lay out in my books, and even most of my gospel principles, are based mostly upon this idea of the higher self. In other words, I say – CHOOSE THE RIGHT!

CHAPTER 17

Moral Weaponry

God does not expect us to be perfect, but he does expect us to <u>try</u> to exercise moral purity for our own sakes at least. This can be shown to us in several ways. The Ten Commandments in the book of Exodus on the Bible is a good place to start. There are many other literary sources of good moral laws. They can also be seen more to be simply good advice from a loving Father.

The onus is always on the receiver of the gifts to determine their ultimate worth. Are you able to accurately discern the value of the gifts that God has given to you? A great gift that one person can give to another is the <u>opportunity</u> for that receiver to show their worthiness in receiving such gifts and that is what our Father does.

In our cases, as human beings, God has given us the opportunity to become independent through our moral agency. That means that we will be a free moral agent, just as He Himself is. We are given commandments out of grace, but we are still free to choose which moral paths we will take. This gift is an opportunity to prove us as righteous weapons in the arsenal of our great God.

In this way, God has also given us opportunities to come to know, through our faith, the qualities of peace and joy and courage with a knowledge that those things will last us all the days of our lives and beyond. He has also given us the opportunity to come to know the truth and to know the difference between right and wrong, which in turn, allows us to become a truly <u>free</u> people.

These moral weapons of God are not usually used for aggressive purposes, but for protective purposes; protection and safety from others who would do us harm and even from ourselves when we let our worst character qualities come to the fore. Some people think that if we live in a righteous and contented state of being at some point that that will be our permanent state. This is not necessarily so. Circumstances are always changing and in the world we live in we will need to seek constant protection for ourselves and for our loved ones.

It does not end when we discover a bit of truth here and a bit of truth there, although that is a good policy. But coming to know the whole truth, as much as we can do so, is the best policy. That can be very difficult to do and I do not believe that everyone can do it by himself, or herself, but I do think that certain people can come very close to doing it. Are you one of those people?

Some of the most ignorant people I know are people who have a reasonable stockpile of truth, but they just do not know how to handle it or they do not want to exercise the sharing policies that go with that truth, for whatever reason. Thus, I say that people who are afraid to use those sharing policies should go out and do it even just once. Then afterwards, see how your testimony of what is true felt inside you when you exercised those sharing policies and expressed your true feelings according to your best reasoning powers.

Dealing with new problems or challenges often involves new kinds of learning and, hopefully, thus, coming to new understandings. That is a good thing. We will always have an enemy of some kind or another pop up, or we will acquire an enemy at some future time during life. This can be a problem for us, but it is not one that should come as a big surprise. The devil tried to tempt Christ, or confound Him when Christ was alive, so He will probably tempt or confound you. In any case, you should be prepared and even know of ways to challenge the common arguments of skeptics.

Enemies may be capable of 'swarming' us at some point in our lives. We must recognize this principle and act upon it or else we may eventually fall victim to those enemies if we are not prepared.

"Satan has demanded permission to sift you like wheat."
- Luke 22: 31

We, as followers of Jesus Christ, may be called upon to protect ourselves AND protect God's other children from destructive forces in the world. This gift of moral weaponry is one that He has given to all men and women and is an opportunity to prove our intelligence and an opportunity to 'give back' to our creator by being obedient and utilizing the righteous weapons that He has given us.

We use moral weaponry for our own sakes, but we can also use it for the sake of other people. I say this because I believe that there are many good people who really want to see the gospel defended in an intelligent and logical way, and even in a loving way.

When I speak of moral weaponry, or morals in general, it should be assumed that I am speaking about absolute morality as opposed to relative morality. True Christians do not believe in relative morality. Absolute morality, however, is all encompassing.

That is the gift that we have been given. It is a knowledge of the truth and a knowledge of righteousness and an <u>opportunity</u> to exercise stewardship over our progeny and over those who may have become 'captive' in the injustices if the world for a variety of reasons. The main reason will probably be because they did not pay heed to the words of God.

Discipleship is our goal. Discipleship means to live good lives as a follower if a Holy Being, but it is also the opportunity to become fair and kind people, sometimes even like 'spiritual police officers', who are in the service of God to serve and protect all people who <u>try</u> to live under the just and divine laws that have been given to us. The choice as to whether or not we will receive that opportunity and act on it will ultimately be ours alone to make.

What gives us the authority to be 'policemen for God'? We don't have that authority, but like traffic policemen, we try to direct people. We 'point the way to God'. We point the way to Christ, but <u>we cannot force God's law</u>s on anyone else. It is the word of God as it has been given to us. His word is His law and hence, our law. What gives us the authority to ask people to recognize the will of God in all things? I say that it is the <u>Holy Priesthood</u> as was spoken of by Jesus.

"I will give unto thee the keys of the kingdom."
- Matthew 16: 19

The Holy Priesthood of God has been in effect since the time of Adam. Again, we are talking about the power of God and how God, according to His wisdom, would like to see His power put into effect among all men and women so that we can be active in delivering truth. This is serious business that directly affects our lives. We are not talking about a couple of cops waiting around to nab somebody in a speed trap.

If we are followers of Christ that does not mean that we should go around admonishing all of the non-believers that we meet. But on the other hand, when the society that we live in goes completely off the rails in a moral sense and lessens the general quality of life for all, then the followers of Christ have a duty to speak up about it and offer healthy alternatives and even to stand apart from society in general if need be.

Will we ever get rejected for our speaking out for what we believe to be right and wrong? Of course we will. Rejection will not kill us though.

Persecution however, may do that, but let us cross that bridge when we come to it. Nevertheless, we can take comfort in the fact that we are in good company and we will also have the knowledge that we never left our friends and neighbors without a warning.

There is not really a logical reason why God should reward us for our good works, whatever those works may be. Shortly before Martin Luther died, a piece of paper containing his handwriting was found in his pocket. Among other words on the paper were these:

"This is true. We are all beggars."

During his lifetime, Luther had come to see the holiness and justice of God. He realized he had no righteousness whatsoever to declare himself acceptable before God. Luther only had Christ. Yet, in having Christ, he had everything: assurance of heaven, peace with God, and a calm heart. Simply clinging to Christ alone Martin Luther was very affective and turned the 1500s Europe upside down.

We are all beggars as Luther said, but we still beg for the salvation of other men and women, and not just ourselves. God will reward us for our concern, but it is only out of love that He rewards us and we never know exactly what those rewards will be. The greatest gifts that He can give us are not things, but opportunities; the opportunities to use our moral weapons and put them into practice so that we can become worthy Christian soldiers and be a useful part of His Kingdom, working to preserve goodness wherever we may find it.

Aside from this great goal, disciples of Christ are also given many other rewards for our diligence and for our righteous integrity. Among His other gifts, are the opportunities for happiness, the opportunities for self-correction, the opportunities to prove our worth, the opportunity to be with our loved ones forever, and the opportunity to obtain Eternal life in His Holy realm that is called Heaven.

"He hath made my mouth like a sharp sword."
- 1 Nephi 21: 2

CHAPTER 18

Righteous Anger

ONE 'POSSIBLE' SOLUTION TO RECLAIM
A LOVED ONE FROM ADDICTION

Some people are successful at stopping their addictive behavior and some are not. Many people do not survive their addictions even when they realize that it is a life or death situation, either of the body or of the soul or both body and soul. That is how powerful a serious addiction can be. There are many programs put into place to help people overcome addictions. This includes 12 step programs, which are often successful.

In my previous books I have laid out some of my own ideas for addiction recovery and I actually worked in an addiction recovery program for two years as a facilitator. I would like to state a new theory that I have on the subject. It is something I call the development of 'righteous anger'.

The term 'righteous anger' can be a misunderstood one. Google, as you may know is a very left wing, politically correct media outlet. They generally believe that a person who believes that some people are more righteous than others is a bigot and an elitist. According to their politically correct stance, that is what they really think. They simply don't understand that some people have good reasons for their righteous anger. That is a very biased and stupid definition of course, but not so fast. I would disagree with that in some cases. I say that some people really are more virtuous and understanding than others.

As proof that some people are more virtuous than others, just ask yourself if you would rather keep company with an honest and honorable person or keep company with someone who was a liar and a thief.

There is good and bad in the world today, and yesterday, and there will be tomorrow too. Anyone with common sense will know what I am talking about. Some people just live by higher standards than others and those people usually want to hold their children or loved ones accountable to those same high principles. It may not be successful one hundred per cent of the time, but if the feel that it is a reasonable and fair thing to do, then I say that that is a valid way of thinking.

Thus, I say that trying to 'induce' self-control in someone else when they desperately need it, is okay. I believe that person who tries to be a benefit to others is much better than one who is called an 'enabler'.

I am not talking specifically about people who get angry with other people and blame them for all of their misfortune or even blame them for their own shortcomings. What I am talking about here is people who are willing and spiritually able to take responsibility for their own actions and try to convince others that such self-discipline is good, and such a person is a good friend and a good influence.

I am referring specifically here to addicts of any kind, that is people who cannot seem to control themselves when it comes to partaking in life destroying, or even soul destroying, activities. I am saying that such people need not be self-loathing, but they might need to <u>get mad at themselves and even feel shame.</u>

What do you do when you cannot resist the thought of indulging in some kind of addictive pleasure like the overuse of alcohol or drugs, or an obsession with sex? There is one thing you can try if more lenient strategies do not do the trick. That is for the person to get mad - at themself. Get very angry even, but let us channel that righteous anger into a direction that is, at least, an <u>honest direction</u>. Tell someone your reasons for feeling the way you do and make sure they understand why you are trying to persuade them into taking responsibility for their actions.

Is your self-criticism going to affect your self-esteem? Maybe. So what? Your self-esteem is going to suffer anyways if you give in to carnal or addictive indulgences. There is a difference between denying what you know to be right and feeling shame. Feeling shame is a corrective measure and correction is a good thing. Denying what you know is right is self-deception and a lie.

If you had a good friend or relative or mentor who you felt you could trust, and they offered you some friendly constructive criticism on your behavior would you appreciate that and take it to heart if it made sense? You should. The worst thing you could do is to downplay your reaction and say that the issue is not important. That puts you in a state of denial. Again, denial is a lie and lying is a tool of the devil.

The second chapter on the Book of Mormon is called Second Nephi. It was authored by Nephi who was the third son of the first prophet Lehi. Nephi was born somewhere around 600 BC.

In chapter 4 of second Nephi, Nephi is grieving over the death of his father and in his writings, he does some self analysis and chastises himself for his weaknesses. He gets mad at himself. He gives praise to God as he pours out his soul, but at the same time, there are points in his writing where he becomes angry with himself and exhibits much humility.

> *"Oh wretched man that I am. Yea, my heart sorroweth because of my flesh; my soul grieveth because of mine iniquities. I am encompassed about because of the temptations and the sins which do so easily beset me."*
>
> *- 2 Nephi 4: 17, 18*

Nephi was a very righteous man and great leader of his people. He was also a smart man and he realized that men and women all have a dual nature. Sometimes people's good nature prevails over their bad nature and sometimes it is vice-versa. Hopefully the good nature will prevail the vast majority of the time, but he knows that when a person slips up there will be a need for self-correction or repentance.

Many readers of that book are surprised when Nephi chastises himself. His righteous mentality causes him to be totally honest and confess the truth about his own human nature. He understands the principle of acknowledging his own weaknesses while in the presence of the God of truth, and he realized that there were times when he came up short when he was <u>not</u> on the same level of that God that had helped him through so much in his difficult life.

Being a righteous man, he must have experienced some pain as he chastised himself. We all have our vulnerabilities or weaknesses or 'uncovered bases'.

By getting mad at himself, expressing regret and confessing his faults on paper (or on metal plates as were used then) Nephi covered his uncovered bases. It probably hurt him, but I suspect he felt much better after he confessed and repented. He did not feel the need to verbally abuse himself, but I suspect that his higher self was very stern with his lower self, which is a good thing.

Nephi begins by expressing his gratitude for the things that God has blessed him with. He reasons that his gratitude should overcome his self-loathing. In verse 26 he describes his regret and sorrow for some of the unholy things he has done:

> 26 *"O then, if I have seen so great things, if the Lord in his*
> *condescension unto the children of men hath visited men in so*
> *much mercy, why should my heart weep and my soul linger*
> *in the valley of sorrow, and my flesh waste way, and my*
> *strength slacken, because of mine afflictions.*

> *27 And why should I yield to sin because of my flesh? Yea, why should I give way to temptations that the evil one should find place in my heart to destroy my peace and afflict my soul? Why am I angry because of mine enemy?*

> *28 Awake my soul. No longer droop in sin. Rejoice, O my heart, and cry unto the Lord, and say: O Lord, I will praise thee forever; yea, my soul will rejoice in thee, my God, and the rock of my salvation.*

In verse 31 he adds:

> *31 O Lord, wilt thou redeem my soul? Wilt thou deliver me out of the hands of mine enemies? Wilt thou make me that I might shake at the appearance of sin?*

These words are not words of anger or complaining. They illustrate Nephi's humility and his passion in wanting to find redemption and in wanting to bring clarity to his own mind and to better understand his own anguish and his wretched condition, so that he may once again find peace in his soul.

It may be difficult to reprimand a loved one for their lack of self-control, but I just think that, in some situations, a reprimand might be exactly what they need. A reprimand is not always a bad thing in some cases. Guilt is also not always a bad thing. Sometimes a reprimand can trigger guilt feelings in a healthy way. Sometimes, a reprimand can be a way of showing someone you care, as long as you try to avoid personal insults and try to discuss things intelligently.

CHAPTER 19

Back to Basics

SUBTITLES:

- ⮑ Rejoice
- ⮑ A Magnificent Event

The following is the text from a talk I gave at my church on July 21, 2019.

Good morning. I would like to bear testimony of the gospel of Jesus Christ and I would ask our Heavenly Father for His Spirit to be here with me as I do that.

Approximately ten years ago the Canadian National hockey team was playing for the World Championship. The team management hired the famous hockey player Wayne Gretzky to be the head coach of the team. The Championship tournament was to be held in Italy.

The players were exceptionally talented, but to the surprise of many, Wayne began coaching the team by having them practice basic skating drills. The sports writers there wondered why he was spending so much time making these highly skilled professional players do skating drills. Wayne explained to the reporters that, "it is always good to get back to the basics". Since Mr. Gretsky's hockey career was slightly more successful than my own, I would defer to his opinion on this. It is always good to, once in awhile, get back to the basics.

So how does this relate to the church? Elder Jeffrey R. Holland, a member of quorum of the twelve Apostles, recently gave a talk where he said, **"the great truth of all eternity is that God loves us."** That 'great truth' might also be called the 'basic' truth. According to Elder Holland (and I hope Mr. Gretzky), it is always good to get back to the basics.

If 'love' is the basic truth of religion let me ask you, do you think that God loves you? Does He love me? Does He love that person sitting beside you? Does He love that person outside this building who is just walking down the street?

I would answer all of those questions with an unqualified 'yes'. The reason I say that is because of a very well known scripture verse given to us in John 3: 16.

> *"For God so loved the world that He gave His only begotten Son that whosoever believeth in Him should not perish, but have everlasting life."*
>
> *– John 3: 16*

So how important a person do you think you are? Lets go right to the top on this. How important are you to God? I will tell you. You are so important that the great Creator of the whole universe sacrificed up His only begotten son, His perfect Son, to suffer and die in order to win <u>your</u> loyalty. That is how important your loyalty is to God and that is how important YOU are to God. If you are able to receive that sacrificial gift, that alone makes <u>you</u> very, very important. Please, never forget that.

So we might ask, are you and I really worthy of that sacrifice? That would be up to each of us to answer individually, but apparently He and His Son, Jesus Christ, both thought that we are worthy enough. Thus, because they are much wiser than I am, I will defer to their opinions.

Sometimes, I get in a position where I have to defend my faith, not only against people who don't like my religion, but people who are atheists and don't like Christianity, or any religion in general. I look upon a doctrinal confrontation with an atheist as being similar to a boxing match. What if you were a boxer and you had a very deadly knockout punch, say a left hook. But what would happen if you never used that knockout punch? You probably would not win many fights. Personally, I have a scriptural knockout punch in the arsenal of my brain and I just told you where it is found in the Bible.

It is found in the scripture I just quoted in John 3: 16 and I would like you to contemplate it again. **"For God so loved the world" that He gave His only begotten son that whosoever believeth in Him should not perish but have everlasting life"**.

This short verse mentions, or implies, a lot of important things. It mentions everlasting life, love, giving, sacrifice, perishing, son ship, Fatherhood, belief, and basically our relationship with our Creator. This short verse gets right down to the basics. Those things are what the gospel of Jesus Christ is basically about. I love it that the scriptures are so succinct. They often sum up very important things in one sentence. And who is the person who would deny or refuse the offer of the gift of Eternal life? I would think it could only be a person who hates life. It may be understandable for someone to hate society, but to hate life? I cannot fathom that. I used to tell my Sunday school students to memorize that verse and where it comes from. That verse is my knockout punch. No one, in good conscience can defend against that principle of truth. If they do deny it they will be denying their own purpose in life. Your opponent may go on punching, but it will be like they are punching themselves in the face.

That short verse allows us to have a testimony that God really does love us. It gives us confidence when we possess that knowledge and we all need confidence in order to continue living with integrity instead of living by silly human pride. God has proven His love for us by His great gift to us of His only begotten Son. It has been done. There is no need to look any further.

This great truth has already been given to us at great expense. Historically, this world had much wickedness in it and it needed to be redeemed. The good news is that that the redemption has already taken place two thousand years ago. It has already happened. It was 'finished'. There is no need to look any further. The only thing that <u>we</u> need to do now is to 'receive' that redemption in our hearts today. <u>What wonderful news.</u>

For those of us who were not alive two thousand years ago, we can receive that redemption today by the process of <u>true belief</u>. When we receive that redemption <u>today</u>, we will be redeemed <u>today</u>. There is no need to look any further. <u>Double wonderful</u>.

Rejoice

There is a hymn was written about that about eight hundred years ago, but I believe that it holds true today in 2019. It says, **"Rejoice. Rejoice. Emmanuel (Jesus) shall come to thee O Israel."**

The people who wrote that hymn understood the relationship between God the Father, His Son Jesus Christ, (the Messiah), and us, who are His people – Israel. By the way, if you want to know how Latter Day Saints, who come from various backgrounds, could become part of the Kingdom of Israel read Jacob 5 in the Book of Mormon that talks about the process of 'grafting'.

That hymn, 'O Come, O Come Emmanuel', also talks about how we need to be set free from Satan's chains. It covers the basics and, remarkably, it was written in the twelfth century before the printing press was invented. Thus, the people at that time were basically illiterate, yet the people knew what the gospel message was all about. They got it. They got the message of the gospel more than, I think, the average person in this modern world of mass communication in which we live today, actually gets it. What does that tell us? It tells me, personally, that a clear understanding of the greatest story ever told is more important than years of book learning and of more value than a hundred university degrees.

Who is Immanuel? Immanuel is Jesus Christ, or Yeshua, as His name was pronounced in His day. Yeshua came to us here once, two thousand years ago, but He also promised that He will come to us again in the future to fulfill the last part of His mission. That part is called the second coming of Christ.

When He comes again, will you and I be prepared for that? Will that time be a time for rejoicing <u>or</u> a time for remorse? For myself, I know that I will <u>only</u> be able to face Him if I have repented of the sins for which I am accountable. Jesus Christ is the only one who has the power to forgive us for those sins. His sacrifice for us all has qualified him to be able to do that. Will my own efforts be rewarded on the day of judgment? I don't know, but I do have the belief that whatever happens, I will personally, be judged fairly.

How do you feel about that? In one word, what would you do if you gained a spiritual witness of that truth by the Holy Ghost? I have a one-word suggestion. That one word begins with R. I am talking about the word REJOICE. It is not difficult unless a person has been steeped in despair or far too long to consider the process of change. It is a glorious passage that was given to us in scripture, so let us REJOICE!

But now it is time for us to reverse the question. Do we love God? Do we love Him with all our heart? How can we show that we love Him? Again, it was written in the Bible in very simple language. It was revealed when Jesus said:

> *"If you love me, keep my commandments."*
> *- John 14: 15*

So you see, it is all very simple. Despite what some people say, the Ten Commandments still apply to us today. If you are obeying the commandments, not lying, not stealing, not coveting, etc. you will be okay. You will be all right. How do you feel about that? In one word, what does owning that precious information make you want to do? The word I am thinking of starts with R. Again, it is… REJOICE!

Another basic part of the gospel is the power of prayer. When we pray we are talking to God. We cannot look Him in the eye when we talk to Him because we probably couldn't handle that. His glory would just be too bright for our mortal eyes to behold. I suspect that it would literally 'nuke us'. Nevertheless, if we cannot look Him in the eye, we should be able to feel of His presence when we pray to Him. In the book of James we read:

> *"Draw nigh to God and He will draw nigh to you."*
> *– James 4: 8*

This is a simple sentence, but one of extreme importance if we want to gain the faith that He really does love us and that we can trust Him. He may not respond to our prayer in the same hour or the same day, but He will respond to us when He feels that we are ready to receive an answer. He will draw nigh to you when you ask Him to, but on His own time. When you draw nigh to Him and He draws nigh to you remember the feeling that is present at that moment. Thus, it will be easier or you to recognize that feeling in the future and proceed accordingly.

And so I ask, will you draw nigh to Him this coming week? And are you drawing nigh to Him right now in this meeting?

One way to draw nigh to Him is to ask Him questions, even on an intimate level. It might take awhile to get an answer, but I find that, personally, if I am clear-headed, I just 'might' receive an answer <u>immediately</u>. The answers to our questions may or may not come from a speaker in a meeting. If we are in a sacrament meeting, and the speaker is boring, even the speaker is me (heaven forbid), <u>an answer on any topic and designed just for you may come into your mind</u>. It will come for the simple reason that you are in the place where you are supposed to be. You are in a Holy place and are there with a humble heart as you partake of the sacrament. For that reason alone God may consent to commune with us. We must be prepared for that.

So we learn from this that our love for our God is mutual and by praying we are free to communicate with him at anytime. How wonderful is that? The God of the universe wants us to talk to Him He enjoys a good two way conversation. In one word, what does that information make you want to do? It starts with R.... REJOICE!

A few moments ago I asked the Lord to allow the Holy Ghost to be with me as I spoke this morning. Did the Lord grant my wish? If He did, then the Holy Ghost will be here with us at this very moment. Because I trust in God's word, I say to you, "It is very possible that the Holy Ghost, or The Comforter' is present here right now in this building"? Thus, I say that, "HE IS HERE RIGHT NOW. ARE YOU READY TO RECEIVE HIM?"

So I look around. Can I see Him? No, I cannot. It is because that is not the way He works. He is not visible, although someday, He definitely will be visible. But there is no good reason we should not be able to <u>feel</u> the presence of the Holy Ghost if we are clean and if we are devoted to His cause of truth and if we are string in our testimony of Jesus. So I ask you, can you feel His presence now? Is He whispering something to you now?

> *"Therefore, it is given to abide in you; the*
> *record of Heaven; the Comforter."*
> *- Moses 6: 61*

This verse says that the Holy Ghost can 'abide in us'. The Holy Ghost is not a personage of flesh and bones, and that is why He <u>can</u> abide in us. Some people may be too timid or too busy or too bored to acknowledge the presence of the Holy Ghost. So let us acknowledge the failure in ourselves to acknowledge Him, or, at least to 'seek for Him'. And let us consider doing more scripture study and more meditation on the matter, and let us do more monitoring of our spirit and more remembering about the times when we actually felt His Holiness in us in the past.

Brigham Young once said that if we attended Sacrament meeting with the right attitude we would have revelations poured upon our heads like water. What wonderful words to hear from a prophet. Thus, I say we should get <u>excited</u> about the prospect of coming to church and partaking of the sacrament. Are you feeling that cool water of revelation this morning? It could be revelation about anything, probably one that will be according to your particular needs. If that is the case, it makes sense that we should ____ (fill in the blank, starts with R) …. That's it… REJOICE!

A Magnificent event

I have another gospel 'basic' that I would like to mention. That is the Atonement of Jesus Christ, which is the link that allows us to have the opportunity to partake of Eternal life with Him and with the Father.

The world is a beautiful place in many ways. There is beautiful scenery, fresh air, and even, in human terms, the beauty of love and kindness that men and women are capable of displaying for one another. These are very beautiful things.

After living a number of years in this world however, I often get the feeling that underneath all the things that go on there is something very sinister lurking. I perceive that there is another lower and secret level where things can get very ugly. It's a realm where cruelty and hate and ignorance are strong and sometimes even dominant in certain settings. When I think about human suffering that goes on there, I see that the beauty and righteousness of this world can actually be eclipsed, in the minds of some people, by the intensity of the ugly and cruel side.

Subsequently, I have come to the conclusion that the world is so wicked at that bottom level that the world itself can only be redeemed, or be justified, by having an experience that is nothing short of magnificent. It would also need to apply to the entire world, and not just a small part of it. It would have to be so magnificent that to know exactly how it worked could very well be beyond our comprehension.

A beautiful sunset, as exhilarating as it may be, will not be enough to redeem the world. An exciting championship football game, where the home team wins, is not enough to justify the existence of the world. Nor is a gripping movie with a happy ending, or a beautifully performed symphony written by a master composer.

If you golf and you practice hard, you might one day, break par, or even get a hole in one. I have never personally experienced that, but I would imagine that it would make a person feel good. But would it be enough to redeem your soul and bring you into God's presence with full confidence? Would it be enough to redeem the world? No.

You might get a degree from a university and that will make you feel good and give you a sense of accomplishment, but will it be enough to redeem you in eyes of the great God who created us? No. Not even the idea of two people in love will be enough redeem us and to save the world from an eventual state of grief and despair.

I say, however, that by the grace of God, and the Atonement of Jesus Christ, **we can be redeemed**. Those are the <u>only</u> two things that can redeem us from a state of misery and doubt and into a state of bliss. It has already been bestowed upon us, and when I say 'us', I include everyone in this room and even everyone in the whole world. We only need to receive it.

At the center of that experience was a sacrifice that was made by a loving Father for the sake of His children. It was a sacrifice that was given out of pure love, a love that was greater than anything that you or I could imagine. It was a story of a Father's love for His Son, a Son's love for His Father, and the love of both of them, even including the Holy Spirit, given to us human beings, who are God's spirit children.

Nothing short of this magnificent sacrifice, with all of the extreme pain endured by an obedient and perfect Son, would be enough to eliminate and stop the growth of evil in our world. Nothing, except that sacrifice will do. Everything else is minor.

This sacrifice is called the 'Atonement'. Many Christian people realize the value of the Atonement, but I perceive that the world in general does <u>not</u> appreciate it and that most people, even some Christians, don't even know what the word means.

> *"For what doth it profit a man if a gift is bestowed upon him, and he receive not the gift? Behold, he rejoices not in that which is given unto him, neither rejoices in him who is the giver of the gift."*
>
> *– Doctrine and Covenants 88: 33*

Any blessing that you have received in your life is somehow a result of God blessing you. I could not tell you exactly how because I do not know you, but I do know a little about how God works and how He blesses us.

So what is a blessing? I looked it up in the dictionary. It said that a blessing is 'the favor of God'. You should be prepared to receive blessings when they happen, and grateful for blessings given to you after they happen. Otherwise those blessings will not happen, or they will not be recognized, which is the same thing as them not happening. When you are grateful, it will strengthen your testimony of the Savior. Thus, you will be able to worship Him. I believe that is what is what 'worship' means – pure gratitude.

If you do not have a testimony of Jesus Christ and His magnificent Atonement, seek one. The information is there and the Holy Spirit is there to bear testimony of it all. If you don't get a testimony, you may possibly find some degree of contentment in your life, but you will never achieve your full potential. Although that might not send you to hell, it will always remain in your soul as an eternal regret. A testimony of the truth is the most valuable thing you can acquire in this life and the next one. It will allow you to grow to your greatest potential and it can bring you Eternal happiness.

His sacrifice must be acknowledged. No matter what things you or I may have accomplished in our lives, financially, romantically, educationally, or whatever our social status is, or whether we may have excelled in sports or in music or theatre or whatever, those things will mean <u>absolutely nothing</u> if that sacrifice, which happened two thousand years ago, is not acknowledged by you. A championship trophy like the Stanley Cup will become just a cheap piece of tin.

Does God have expectations for you? He has expectations or all of us, otherwise He would not have sent us here. But if we should find ourselves in a land of spiritual desolation, and we do sin, we must always remember one thing. That is that God is quick to forgive when we sincerely repent, and, basically, say that we are sorry and we will try not to do it again.

For the lesser sins, a heartfelt, 'sorry about that' may suffice. For the more serious sins it might take more than that, beginning with a trip to the bishop's office, but the Lord does not want us to sit and stew in our sins and our guilt. That is because He knows that that time is a good time for one of Satan's minions to step in and whisper to us something like – "oh, look what you did. You're such a terrible person. How can you live with yourself?"

No. God does not want that to happen, so He is quick to forgive. That is a sign of His grace and we should always be prepared to <u>receive</u> His grace.

Behold this beautiful chapel in which we sit with our fellow disciples - those who come here because they want to commune with Him and they want to learn of Him. Behold – the scriptures – the words of

God that have somehow, made their way through this wicked world through the centuries that we might learn of Him.

How can you witness God's grace and forgiveness and not love God with all your heart? And yet there may be some people who will throw the Father's gifts back in His face and refuse to accept them. Who those people are is not up to me to judge, but the Father knows who they are and the people themselves know who they are and it has been written that the final destiny of those people is to 'perish'. (2 Peter 3: 9) You cannot get much more final than that.

Christ suffered a lot of pain in His life both on the cross and in the Garden of Gethsemane, where He bled from every pore. It was more pain than you or I could even imagine. Nevertheless, I belief He felt more love for you and me than the pain that he was suffering. Thus, I say, **His love for us was even greater than His pain.** Is that love justified? Are we worthy of it? Christ asked the Father to forgive us and, according to my understanding, the Father did so. Because the Father is more all-seeing than I am, and more righteous too, I will defer to His opinion and be Eternally grateful for it.

Personally though, I cannot see how we would be worthy of it. But apparently God does think we <u>are</u> worthy of it. So, I can only repeat the words of a beautiful hymn: "I stand all amazed at the love Jesus offers me." So if Christ's love for us was greater than the intense pain He was feeling, shouldn't our love for our fellow disciples, who are sitting around us right now, be a greater cause than resolving the comparatively low pain and worries that we are personally dealing with on the world today?

One of the main commandments is to love our neighbors, so let us go forward this week and attempt to do that in whatever way we can. If your efforts aren't making an 'earth-shaking' difference, don't worry or fret about it. Your time to fully prove yourself will come.

So let's get back to the basics like Elder Holland said and love one another and worship God. To me, the word 'worship' could be defined as simply exercising gratitude for the many gifts we have been given. It is also a matter of loyalty.

"The crowning characteristic of love is always loyalty."
- Jeffrey R. Holland

You have, for some reason, been given the true and full gospel of Jesus Christ. In one word, what are you going to do about it? It starts with 'R'... If you don't know, figure it out. I have given you enough hints.

So in closing I will state the purpose of the coming of Jesus. It goes:

"And suddenly there was with the angel a multitude of the heavenly host praising God and saying. "Glory to God in the highest and on earth peace, goodwill toward men."
- Luke 2: 13,14

That is a verse that is usually read at Christmas time, but it is <u>not</u> limited to Christmas time. It is more than that. It is the basic purpose of life.

And I would add, as the great Wayne Gretsky might say, it is a good thing to "get back to basics." It is also a good thing to remember the 'basic truth' that you are a child of God.

CHAPTER 20

Bob's Obbs #2 (Random thoughts)

People should be free to believe what they want to believe, but it is impossible to really accept all religious doctrines because some doctrines might contradict other doctrines. It is not a sin to be critical of other religions if their doctrines do not make any sense. Thus, it is a sin to accept false religion, or no religion, in the name of tolerance. People will often do that though. Why? I suspect it is because they just do not have a strong enough passion for the truth.

Some Christians think that because they might have a knowledge of the gospel, they are the only ones God cares about. This is a mistake. God cares for all people.

Some secular people treat religious people with disdain, but I believe it is the truly religious people who actually hold the world together. Without them the earth would have been pulled out of its orbit a long time ago.

I have my own religion, but I am tolerant of all religions; except, that is, for the ones that tend to breed pathological murderers.

The most important question we can ask about religion is: 'Does God's church really exist now on the earth and if so, which one is it?' This is not a contest to see who can get the right answer. It should simply be a mutual quest by all men and women of all races and origins to seek and to find the one that is most aligned with sensibility and truth.'

I believe that the truth can be found, but most people do not really want to look for it mainly because, if they actually find it, it just might 'cramp their style'.

Too many religions worship 'a book' instead of the inspiration that brought the book into being and the Spirit found within the book.

It does not matter what a person has achieved in the world or how many degrees they have from universities. If they do not understand who Jesus Christ was, and is, they simply do not understand life. People may accomplish many things concerning money, education, a good career, romance, etc., but if they never acknowledge that sacrifice that was made for them two thousand years ago on the cross, their accomplishments will be worth absolutely nothing.

Try to be <u>active</u> in the pursuit of things that matter. Stay close to the good Shepherd. The wolves are always out there and are watching. They know our weaknesses better than we do. They remember how we helped their cause in times past. The Good Shepherd is the only One who has the power to make them shrink away by His presence and even by His name.

Christians have been accused of being dreamers because they believe in an unseen spiritual ideal. From my experience, most of them are not dreamers, but are the most reality-based people I have ever known.

As Christians, we should always try to remember that we are in a <u>yoked</u> relationship with Jesus. That does not mean that I am just sitting in the wagon while He does all the pulling.

Any political argument should be a matter of logistics. Either a principle works or it doesn't work and some things just work better than other things. Thus, aside from faith, true intelligence and open-mindedness are always big factors.

There are many people who have suffered or died from the exercise of political correctness (IE: mob rule), including Jesus Christ Himself. So watch out for anyone who assumes that they are more righteous and charitable than the next person.

Some people say it is not appropriate to mix politics and religion. Perhaps that may have been true at one time, but in the twenty first century we live in a different world than the one people lived in fifty years go. Today, politics and religion cross paths every day. Moral issues like gay marriage and abortion are two examples of that. We have every right to express our personal opinions.

The status quo in our time has changed. While some people want to preserve freedom and individual initiative, there are others who wish to trample all over it and allow the government, (the state) and the academic elites to control matters. Where those people get their faith in the infallibility of the state from, I have no idea, certainly not from history. But if that is what they believe, they have sunk to a level of dogmatism that an extremely strict religion might have had in centuries past.

To employ eternal vigilance in overcoming problems may be necessary, but it is easier when it is a <u>team</u> effort. Choose your team wisely. Be sternly vigilant because the devil roams the earth and he even walks in the institutes of higher education, and lower education, and in the halls of legislative assemblies.

Everyone's opinions are based upon what they know. In that way, everyone's opinion may be called valid. On the other hand, we know that not everyone's opinions are valid. Therefore, it follows that the truth or <u>the validity of a person's opinion is mostly based upon the correctness of the information that they possess,</u> and sometimes that information is not totally correct.

To explore principles of truth in our lives, we also need to have knowledge about the people who desire to take the truth away from us, and the knowledge of why they would wish to do that. I believe that the reasons why certain adversaries wish to do us harm often may have their origins in a time that was well before our present mortal life.

Even though truth is constant, the context in which it may be found is not necessarily constant and might change. It can be fluid, but we should know how to adapt to those changes when we become aware of them. We should be able to adapt to that fluidity while consistently holding on to our foundational principles.

We need to grasp precepts of knowledge at the moment they present themselves to us. Inspired thoughts are called 'revelations' and we must try to internalize a revelation the moment it enters our mind and write it down. That is because if a true answer to an important question is ignored, the answer to it may disappear and never return to us.

The best way to learn how we might live a happy and productive life is to inquire from the Author of life itself, who is living still, and will always be living. He lives in a realm of light not a realm of darkness.

A lack of information is like a vacuum. At a higher level of intelligence the vacuum will be filled by truth. At a lower level of intelligence it will be filled by emotions, fears, sensationalism and <u>gossip</u>.

Wisdom is just as important, if not more important, than what we call 'love'. This is because wisdom will allow us to see the true reality of love and when we do not see the truth behind love, it can lead us into all kinds of errors.

Seek the will of God in all things and then have the courage to act on it. Wisdom comes first. Courage comes second.

I have read the writings of many people who I consider to be wise. I picture them to be firstly good humored and gentle in nature. I have met wise people who have been bold, but I have never met a person I considered to be wise who was an angry person at heart.

Ironically, having pride in one's intellect is not that smart. Earthly wisdom is often difficult to acquire or maintain. There are other faculties that can work better for our own good. Having spiritual discernment is one. Having a sense of self worth is another. An ability to work well with other people is another. Having a love for life is another.

Every morning when we wake up, we step out of a dream state, or a slumber state, and then we identify ourselves to ourselves. Will we identify ourselves in the flesh (our job, our status, our image, our nationality, etc.) or will we identify ourselves in the spirit (children of God with divine potential)?

It is a careless person, or a careless culture, that causes, or allows, people to pass by wisdom. If young people do not want to possess wisdom, they will not gain a love for life. When they do not possess a love for life, they will not have true respect for anybody or anything. When they do not have respect, they cannot really love anything or anyone.

The best knowledge that one can possess is to know how to create personal happiness on a consistent basis. A simpleton can be richer than a millionaire if he, or she, knows how to do this.

Knowledge includes action. We may know where the light switch is on the wall and what it can do, but that does not matter if we choose never to turn it on.

As humans, our great capacity for making wonderful discoveries that make positive contributions to society is only exceeded by our immense capacity for self-justification and making up excuses.

A 'realization' of anything is a true 'intellectual event'. When any new knowledge is gained, the personal implications of it should be written down, shared and pondered. This is a **'realization event'**. Celebrate it and turn it into true knowledge.

I believe that it is not those who possess the most truth and knowledge who are most favored by God. It is <u>those who make the best use</u> of whatever truth and knowledge that they have been given.

We do not need revolutions. We need revelations.

The truth is forever at rest. The proclamation of truth is never at rest.

The truth is not our enemy, but our greatest ally. I am not talking about cold, hard facts, but the warm spirit of truth. If it is not incorporated into our cause, it will be outside of our cause. If we are not fighting for it, we will be fighting against it.

The mutual quest to find the truth goes out the window when one person deliberately tries to misrepresent the opinions of another. This strategy is often seen in political debates.

If you ever feel that you have found the truth, you must face the distinct possibility that truth can be a delicate thing and that many of the people you know will not accept it. Many of them will say in effect, 'you're ideas are not welcome here'. This can apply to certain family members, friends, work associates and people you may have known all your life.

In these modern times temptations are all around us. There are, basically, two things that you can do that are most effective in avoiding temptations. The first is to pray regularly and ask your heavenly Father for help. The second thing is to stop thinking about your temptation or distraction and then get up and DO SOMETHING GOOD. You might start that by giving service to other people or by reading uplifting books and increasing your knowledge of spiritual things.

CONTEXT: You need to let the space you occupy shine. You don't need to shine yourself; especially if you are old and/or handicapped, but you've got to let the space that you are in shine. (Its all about attitude). Its all about your context.

CHAPTER 21

The Seventy Percent Club

Have you ever felt happy? I don't mean overjoyed. I mean alive, focused and at peace with the world and with yourself; hoping to find an opportunity to share your good feelings with others. On the feel good scale of 1 to 100 I am talking about somewhere around the 70 to 90 percent mark.

I will take that as a 'yes'. That's good.

Perhaps you are feeling very good right now. Are you between 70% to 90% on the happiness scale? If not, perhaps you have a memory of when you last felt like that. Perhaps that was yesterday. Perhaps it was last year. All I want to know is if you can recall some portent of that feeling.

Now what I want you to do is to examine that feeling if you are feeling it right now, or else by recalling it, and then actually trying to sustain that feeling.

Right now.

Take a minute to count your blessings or think about something positive that makes you feel good and try to feel that feeling. Aim your emotions, or your recollections of your emotions for the two thirds mark that is 70 percent or thereabouts. Take a few moments if need be.

It should be fairly simple for anyone to summon up such a feeling in themselves and maintain it for, at least, a little while. The reason that I ask you to do this is because that is the goal of a club that I have formed. It is called 'The Seventy Per Cent Club' and I would like to tell you about it.

The Seventy Percent Club is a social club where people get together to talk in a forum setting about issues they experience in their daily lives, either at work or with their families; experiences that have an effect on their moods. The goal of the group is for people from all walks of life to express their opinions and try to come up with acceptable solutions to any problems that anyone might have in the way they react to things that happen to them, good and bad. It does not need to be about personal things, a discussion could be on general topics chosen beforehand; even topics from this book. They do this in a way that is amicable and promotes friendliness and the free interchange of ideas, while maintaining a positive outlook of, at least, sixty seven percent, or 66 2/3, (rounded off to seventy). People may end up agreeing to disagree, but they should not leave a meeting feeling bitter in any way and without trying to hit that magic number of 70%.

Extraordinary good feelings come when people are consistently at a minimum of seventy percent on the happiness scale. You might think this would be difficult to accomplish in a discussion, but if it is based upon a philosophy of faith and the moderator has the right skills, it is not difficult to summon good feelings in a group setting. We just need to remind ourselves that the option to be happy is always there and anyone can make that leap when they need to by their own free choice. Aside from reminding ourselves of that capability we all have, we must also turn away from those things that would cause us to descend from that mark. And there are many of them. Nevertheless, club members should always commit to staying the course.

Seventy percent. That is the mantra that should be consistently brought into our minds when things get a little rough. That is the minimum. If you are feeling a little down right now, repeat after me please, "Seventy percent! Seventy percent!" You can even make it eighty or ninety percent if you wish.

You may get motivated, you may not. Either way, you have nothing to lose. If it doesn't work, try it again later when things pick up a little.

If you are a sincere person who desires to be happy, then by repeating this mantra every time you start to feel a little down, you will recall the mission you have set for yourself as a member of this club. By going to a place where we talk about the actual properties of happiness and love, we must, at some point discuss religion. That is because religion, by definition, is an analysis of mankind's search for happiness. By doing things and talking at a truthful level, I think you will find that you will, by some mysterious process, find it much easier to make the 'happiness leap'. You will find yourself becoming more confident and more spiritual and thus, more able to automatically be transported to the seventy and ninety percent range.

It stands to reason, as I have said, that if there are certain thoughts or activities that you are engaged in at the time of your emotional discomfort, then you must drop those activities or those thoughts and do something else, realizing that it is the thoughts you are entertaining that are part of the problem, if not the whole problem. If you can dismiss all bad thoughts and bad actions from your presence, then it is almost certain that you will, by your own leadership qualities and with the gentle nudging of the good spiritual influences in your life, hit your goal of seventy to ninety percent and start to feel better immediately.

The trick is though, to stay at the highest level you can for as long as possible.

In the Seventy Percent Club we like to socialize and share ideas. We communicate with each other on a fairly regular basis and continually remind each other about our common and universal goal as members. That goal is to willfully put ourselves in a happy mood every minute of every day. We do this to help us feel good about this life we live and also to help others feel good being around us. Having conversations with people who are kind, honest, and have a passion for life and for people is, I find the best way to facilitate the clearing of your mind so that you can, at least, catch a glimpse of what happiness is all about.

Thus, some us members are Christians, but some members may not be. In any case, we are not afraid to share religious ideas. In fact, although it is not spoken about, we demand, in an unspoken way, that members who come to our 70% meetings be mature enough and courageous enough to face a different variety of ideas as long as they might possibly contribute to the emotional well being of everybody in the group.

We aim to exercise these good feelings that we summon to the point where such feelings become habitual. It is very simple to do and it works. And it doesn't cost anything. It is so simple that some people might tend to take it lightly. That would be a mistake because they may be dismissing something that will actually improve their quality of life and make a difference in their outlook on many things.

All that is required is a sense of gratitude for the good things you have and an optimistic spirit. A little bit of faith certainly helps too. Cynicism and constantly playing devil's advocate is definitely not in the equation. I might also mention that a good moderator for our meetings is very important. That would be a man or a woman who can keep everybody focused on our mutual goal, which is:

"Seventy per cent. Seventy percent. At least"

Why seventy to ninety percent? Because we know that during the course of an average day some bad things will probably happen, or some frustrating things, or some uncomfortable things, or some stressful things, or some downright nasty things.

When such things happen, it is very difficult to retain your seventy percent goal, because, on a bad day, you will probably find yourself sinking downwards. However, you should <u>try</u> not to sink below the 50% mark, and at all costs, try to avoid the 33% mark.

Always try to stay above the fifty per cent mark no matter what. Linger around the fifty one percent mark for as long as you wish, but don't let yourself sink below the fifty percent level. If you should happen to sink below the fifty percent mark all is not lost. If you should happen to fall below the 33% mark though, then you are in serious trouble. You are floundering in that bottom 1/3 of existence, then some strong motivation and inspiration, if not intervention, will be required to get you out of that hole.

At 49% you will be wading in dirty water. At 33% it is like going below the surface of the water when you are swimming against a strong current. You can survive there, but you do not want to reside there. The water at those lower depths is very dirty. If you are immersed in it, you will find that you will not be able to breathe properly. Your beautiful lungs will not be happy because you will be largely cut off from your spiritual oxygen supply.

It is our belief in the Seventy Percent Club that we can help people feel better about themselves and about the world around them and we should make a point of aiming for that whenever we can. The thing is we've got to be at least at the fifty one percent mark if we are going to be able to be somewhat contented and able to rise above our natural tendencies that cause us to become complacent and to be without hope and thus, feel a sense of despair.

When people's happiness levels get below the thirty three percent mark, it is like talking to someone who is under water. They can't hear you. Their ears are plugged with the water of the world, or a feeling of self-pity, or a resentment of some kind. If you want to help them you must wait until they come up for air and poke their head above the water. At fifty one percent, you can talk to them. You can even lift them into the boat where they will feel safe and be able to breathe the fresh air in a clean environment.

So <u>fifty one percent</u> is the acceptable minimum in a stressful situation, but as an overall average fifty one is simply not good enough for those of us members who have it as their stated goal to try to live life to the fullest. Therefore, seventy to ninety percent is what we aim for.

That extra one percent in the fifty one percent example is like one higher rung on a ladder. It enables you to go up <u>to fifty two per cent</u> once you get feeling confident. From there it can slowly proceed upwards.

JACOB'S LADDER

The increase in our good feelings may come in small increments (like one per cent at a time), but there is also another factor. I personally call it the 'Jacob's ladder factor'. In that story in the Old Testament of the Bible, Jacob's ladder is interpreted as <u>'the bridge between heaven and earth'</u>. That means that the Lord can provide a ladder to ascend to a higher spiritual/emotional level out if the goodness of His heart. Thus, by the grace of God, it is actually possible for our ascendancy to come in larger increments, and even immediately. Such a gift can happen slowly or happen instantly if we are spiritually attuned to receive it.

This concept is a landmark concept to me because it marks a time when the spiritual/theological process mingles with a modern psychological process in perfect harmony. It might take some time for a human being to reach that point, but it can happen and when it does happen, it should be clear that it is a special gift that comes from above.

There is another thing you should know about the club and that is concerning the other end of the scale - ninety per cent and up. We recognize that the top 10% on the quantitative scale of joy is a state that is given to us as a gift, <u>but</u> it can be a bit of a precarious state. A person may be in a state of rapture, but in that state, they can also be very vulnerable. That it can be seen as a state of ecstasy, which is wonderful, but it can be a state where a man or woman, by themselves, might be too vulnerable and not able to handle it properly because there may be an invisible precipice in the picture.

In many cases it takes a high degree of acquired wisdom to be able to sustain one's level headedness or rationality. There needs to be a balance in attaining that mark simply because of our vulnerability as human beings. Thus, as we approach that area of the top ten percent with anticipation, we also should proceed with some caution.

The ninety to one hundred percent mark is a crossover point. That's the place where the lowest part of divinity meets the highest part of humanity. It is, in a sense, sacred ground, and that can be overwhelming, even to a person with a good knowledge of sacred things. Individuals may not know how to respond in a way that would do justice to that space and to comprehend it and fully appreciate the exquisite feelings that can be found there. We should always keep the word 'humble' in mind when our 'cup runneth over' as it says in an old hymn.

There is a danger that that space will be underappreciated. In order that you be 'grounded' properly, a person should not 'go there' without an identifiable guiding spirit or with a good friend whom you know you can trust; possibly both. At the same time, the voyageur that dares to enter into this blissful state should have two things going for them. Those are an absence of guile of any kind, and a spirit of gratitude and humility.

I would like to expand a little on this faith that I spoke about earlier. In my younger days, if I was able to arrange a life's plan and a philosophy without Jesus Christ at the center of it, I probably would have gone that route. That is because, in my natural youthful state I was a prideful sort of person and I liked to do things my own way. For me, that attitude proved to be lacking at best and disastrous at worse.

As I have matured, I have found that I cannot enter into a plan for happiness, without bringing a perfect mentor (IE: Jesus Christ), into the equation. I believe this process will be confirmed and even accelerated when you study the stories and the words of Christ in the scriptures. I could not honestly help someone else try to find happiness without bringing Christ into the equation and I will try to explain why this is so.

I had a religious conversion some years ago in which I simply realized that the mission of Jesus Christ was a divine one and a foreordained one. I also came to realize that, because of His Atonement, all knowledge that I seek and all truth that I might possess and all authority I claim must first be sanctified or endorsed by Him or by His appointed messengers.

Therefore, I seek His guidance in all I do and this comes to me by the presence of the Godhead who is also known as the Holy Ghost, who is also known as the Comforter. I believe that Jesus is actually alive today and works with the Holy Ghost to give wisdom and comfort to those who need it and who ask for it.

In the Seventy Percent Club, that is the philosophy, or theology, that we approve of.

I do not wish to force my beliefs on anyone else; I simply seek for like-minded people, and people who are willing to learn and willing to to share ideas. If anyone disagrees with my perspective, that is their prerogative. They can always seek their own ways of finding happiness and I sincerely wish them luck.

I will not try to force or intimidate anyone into adopting my belief system, but I do want him or her to feel happy about their lives because that is the reason we are all here. If we are not happy, then all else is irrelevant. So we should go forth together with some kind of plan and encourage all to actively seek answers to metaphysical and religious questions with an open mind, and on their own time, as long as they do not dawdle too long. Our time is precious.

So this faith is the most valuable component of the things we speak about and reflect upon. I believe that with a certain amount of faith, the ability of a person to willfully jump from, say a fifty to a seventy percent level of joy is increased greatly. With faith our capabilities and our confidence can be greatly increased. Hence, it is easier for a person to reach their happiness quotient by using their faith as a springboard. Find out for yourself. Experiment on the principles. Seventy percent is the goal; whether you can go there in an instant or whether it takes a little more time.

I sometimes suspect that the 70% Club may not be of use to people who are always optimistic and focused and happy. "Good for them", I say. In any case, it is an excellent thing for people like me who, I will admit, can get easily discouraged, or downhearted, on some days.

It is truly a 'self-help' program, but it is also a 'help-others' program. It is <u>effective</u> for two reasons; number one, because it is simple. It does not usually require any therapy or over-analysis. If anyone, in the course of a discussion, gets too personal or dogmatic or over analytical, they should be corrected by the moderating speaker.

Number two: it is fairly specific, inasmuch as attitudes and emotions can be specific. Seventy percent is the goal. Aim for it and when you hit the mark, then aim for a little higher, eighty or ninety per cent. Even if you come up short, you should still hit seventy. It's win/win. If you find that you cannot hit seventy, just try your best, but make sure you are not below fifty%.

If you <u>do</u> sink below thirty three per cent though, do not despair. Just remember one thing. It is in your nature that you will float to the surface again soon as long as you have some measure of <u>hope</u> in you. All it takes is a little thing called 'time'. I am talking about the time it takes to let the Holy Spirit buoy you up so you can rise to the surface again.

Sometimes it might be best to be by yourself for a while until that happens. You may even want to put yourself in 'voluntary quarantine', so to speak. When you do float back up to the surface, the members of the Seventy Percent Club will be there to assist you in any way we can so you might get back up to seventy and beyond. In this way the group can also act as a prayer group for those who are going through difficulties. Those people who are going through difficulties are also invited to pray which will give them the opportunity to connect with the Spirit alongside the other members.

The discussions and communications that we like to have in this club, whether meeting in person or online is of value for three reasons that I can think of right now.

One, it gives a person an opportunity to articulate how they are doing on their quest to become consistently happy, in a noticeable sense. Articulation, verbal or written, is always a good thing. It reinforces feelings and ambitions on a higher level. Articulation about positive feelings helps to entrench positive feelings in our characters.

Two, it gives a person an opportunity to express opinions about philosophical issues and ideologies in forums that are specifically designated for that. There are lots of people who have good ideas and suggestions and good questions about all kinds of things, but they have nobody to talk to them about so those ideas might easily just wither on the vine. Then those people end up feeling that their ideas are not that good because nobody seems to want to listen to them. In reality though, they may be great ideas. They just need a person with good listening skills to hear them. Our club members have it as their stated duty to promote good listening skills.

The third reason is that like attracts like. Happy people are most happy when they are around other happy people. Meeting for a good and common purpose and discussing uplifting things can bring a good spirit into a meeting and everyone will leave in a better mood. Disagreements are tolerated in the club, but contention is not. An air of civility prevails in the club, but people are always free to voice their opinions. They would be well advised though to be prepared to back up those opinions with some amount of reason.

The people in this club are intelligent and will not accept philosophies or opinions that are based upon pure assumptions. Another thing to remember is that some people have a tendency to complain about their personal problems and sometimes on a level where other people either don't want to know about them and/or they are not in a position where they can do anything about them. If that is the case, our meetings could turn into a 'pity party' and we do not want to 'go there'. Good advice is fine, and sympathy is good, but time spent on pitying can be counter-productive.

Yes, the Seventy Percent Club takes on the seemingly impossible task of trying to measure (in approximate terms) an individual's happiness quotient and to <u>obtain</u> that 70 to 90% ratio of joy in our hearts on a daily basis. This is so that we might be more effective and productive in all we do and to make more contributions for good in all of our relationships and endeavors. These efforts will better enable us to enjoy life to the fullest.

We recognize that like attracts like. Joy attracts more joy. But on the opposite end, sadness attracts more sadness. We recognize that there are many people who will not accept our exuberance and some may even resent us for it. That is not our problem. It is their problem.

This is not a fool's paradise. We recognize the words of Paul the apostle when he talked about the necessity for patience and long suffering. Nevertheless, there is another commandment from Jesus Himself that says "be of good cheer". Thus, it is always good to monitor ourselves and to know when we are 'in the safe zone' of that good cheer and when we are not. Good cheer is not a brash thing. Happiness and cheer are very delicate things and can even be subtle things.

<u>Good cheer is not the advancement of the boldest part of you. It is the advancement of the gentlest part of you.</u> Acknowledging when we are in that zone makes it easier for us to appreciate it and to 'increase the shining moments'.

So that is the basic outline for the Seventy Percent Club. If you are interested, read on. If you want to become a member, let us know. You might even decide to start your own chapter. If you are not a 'club joining' type of person, that's fine, but just try to have faith that life is good. Reinforce it by reading scriptures and standing in holy places.

And, once in a while, say this mantra to yourself - **"Seventy per cent, seventy per cent, seventy per cent!**

Chapters for our club can be set up anywhere by anyone. If you wish to participate in our forums, there is no cost. If you wish to officially join the club and receive our newsletter and get a chance to make posts on the bulletin board, the membership is twenty dollars per year. This fee is to cover administration costs like perhaps acquiring a rental space for meetings.

All expenses will be accounted for and published. It is a non-profit organization. The fee also acts as a deterrent to people who would cause trouble by making inappropriate posts. Such people will not pay twenty bucks to cause trouble when they can do it on other sites for free. We may even spend some money to advertise our club as we want people to know there is a 'happiness club' out there that they can attend.

If you are interested in the 70% Club and in being an official "seventy per center", please contact: bob.sandwiches@gmail.com. Thank you and we hope to hear from you.

CHAPTER 22

The Baha'i Church and One World Government

Many years ago when I was going to University of Manitoba, a once respected university, which has since fallen from grace because of the establishment of a leftist administration that took over in the school. Such a thing was very common in many universities around the end of the last century, and is true to this day even with all of the social upheavals that we see around us. Dangerous ideologues have literally taken over the university system.

One day I was walking around the common area of the school and I noticed that there was some people there manning an information booth. They said they were from the Baha'i church and wanted to pass along some information to students. One of the main ideas they were pushing was their desire to convince the students to promote the establish of a 'one world government'. Being young and stupid at the time, I agreed with their initial argument that having a united front would probably make the whole world a more peaceful place. They had a petition there for people who agreed with that notion to sign. I signed the petition.

A few weeks later I received a letter welcoming me as a new member of the Baha'i church. That was a surprise to me. I believed in world peace, but I never had any intention of joining a church, especially one that I knew nothing about. Because of some spiritual experiences, I did believe in God, but I really had no idea what His, or Her, true nature was. I decided to do a little studying on the history of that church.

The books that I read said basically that the church began in Persia, which is now the country of Iran. They believed that early prophet of their church, who was named Baha'u'llah, was the true messiah for the world and even above the status of Jesus Christ. This new Messiah spent most of his life in prison where he wrote many books of alleged scriptures. I found the stories and the writings of his interesting and the people were very friendly, but I thought I would hold off on making a final judgment on them.

It the end, I found that I did not have enough spiritual experiences that would cause me to join that church, so I left it alone. I went through many years without having any church to put my faith in and I felt that that was not a healthy thing. I wanted to come to know God, but I knew that I lacked the necessary knowledge to do that. I was raised for the most part in the United Church, but I did not find the solid answers that I needed that would cause me to pursue that avenue.

It wasn't until years later, when I almost drowned in the Pacific ocean one day, that I came to a decision. I believed that God Himself was probably responsible for saving me from drowning that day. I was so relieved that I told God out loud on that beach that I did not know where to find the true church that could explain His doctrine to my satisfaction, but if I ever did find it, then I would definitely join that church. Another twenty years went by without me noticing any dynamic signs about the true church. Along the way, I became involved in the music business and, sadly, had begun to develop a serious liking for alcoholic beverages. Thus, I did not pursue my interest in religion nearly as much as I should have.

One summers day about thirty years ago, a couple of young missionaries from the Church of Jesus Christ of latter Day Saints knocked in my door.

They said that they had the full gospel of Jesus Christ and a book that was called the Book of Mormon that was <u>translated</u> by the first prophet of their church. His name was Joseph Smith. I asked them where Joseph got the book from and they said that an angel gave it to him.

Ooookay. I thought I heard a bell ring in the distance. Could that have been a 'looney alert'?

The missionaries explained many things that I did not know about and the answers for even some questions that I had never thought to ask. One night, a year and a half later and after much study, I actually fasted and prayed to find an answer to the question of whether the church was the true church or not.

The Spirit of the Holy Ghost gave an answer to me that night. I, along with my nine year old son were baptized into the church and I have never looked back since then.

I asked many more questions as the young missionaries visited my house often on Marjorie Street in a suburb called St. James. We had some lively discussions. Over time I received much more knowledge and I became quite fascinated by those things that took place in the beginning church which was located Easter United States in the early part of the nineteenth century.

I have been studying religion now for over thirty years and the reason I told the story about the Baha'is and their desire for a one-world government is to explain how young people can be persuaded by the appeal of an ideology.

A one-world government is one goal of the Bahia church. That kind of church has never been established in all of history although there have been some churches who have tried. I don't think it ever will be established because there are simply too many diverse opinions in the cultures and religions of the world and many of those opinions can have contradictory doctrines behind them.

That is, I suppose, mainly because of the hardness if the hearts of men and women and their inability to find answers about the purpose of life and also because of the understandable fear of charlatans who would lead the people astray. This idea is explained more fully in the scriptures, including the Bible and the Book of Mormon, which is a book that I now view as a second witness of Jesus Christ.

The initial impulse to put any faith in a one-world government, for me, was sparked by the idea of investigating the possibility of people trying to organize a government that would take care of any political disputes that might arise. Yes, it was naive of me, but it seems that is not uncommon in this world and is even happening today.

I came to the conclusion that it was an erroneous notion. Trying to establish a one-world government in the United States would displace the American Constitution, which I believe to be one of the most intelligent political documents in the history of the world, and which came about through much wise deliberation from various leaders and through much effort too. Other nations, to their credit have tried to create a very similar kind of constitution for themselves, by which they might benefit as the U.S.A. did. .

The idea of using a one-world government to run the world struck me as unacceptable to say the least. It reminded me of the Dalai Lama and the Tibetan monks. Those Tibetans refused to keep an army of trained soldiers because if their pacifist philosophy. That may have been noble of them, but I think that it was also was quite naïve of them. In any case, I believe that it was all well intentioned.

As a result of their refusal to provide any opposition, the Communist government in China soon after that invaded Tibet and strict laws were made that prevented the freedom of religion in Tibet. It was sad, but the people were literally held captive and the Dalai Llama, who is their leader now, was forced to travel around the world begging money from other countries so that the Tibetan people could survive.

Years later, my studies on religion led me to take a strong interest in politics, and especially on the notion of individual freedom, which I believe to be a God-given right. I studied political matters for many years including the differences between left wing thinking (communism essentially) and right wing thinking (capitalism essentially).

After more study I finally came to a conclusion about which argument I would side with. I became a conservative; much to the chagrin of my siblings who were all entrenched in socialist ways of thinking and were the bearers of very narrow minded and ill-founded arguments.

As I said at the time, it was not the appeal of capitalism that convinced me to become a conservative, but it was the wrongheadedness, lies, virtue signaling, and viciousness of the left-wingers that repulsed me so much. Sometimes the political discussions I had with people were not pleasant, but that thinking and debating did bring much more clarity to my mind about politics and about people's motives.

I had learned that a central government that had much power would always force their will on the population through bureaucrats and a strong army. Thus, their ideals would be doomed to fail, not only occasionally, but **one hundred per cent of the time**. I also think that history backs me on that idea.

I must say that my point in this essay is a political one and not a religious one. I believe that people should be free to choose their own religion no matter what, (unless it happens to be a religion that breeds pathological murderers.) Also, all of the religious people who I know believe in that same freedom.

I believe that the Baha'i people who I met in my youth were fine people. My problem is with the notion of a 'world government'. That is something that is being promoted even today by leaders in both the east and the west. There are many different religions in the world and some of them have very strict doctrines attached to them. The people in those strict religions do not usually take kindly to compromising their sacred principles. Under a world government, people would eventually be forced to compromise those principles. Either by the world bureaucracy or by the 'world army' would enforce that dictate. (I.E. the United Nations?)

Thus, I predict that if a world government should come to pass, that unwillingness to compromise would lead to more bloodshed, bombings and wars than we have ever seen before.

Thus, at present, I admonish all young people to be patient, listen to other points of view, and think clearly, before making a decision that will affect the future of your particular country, or state, or province, or your family and that will also affect the prosperity and freedom of your children and grandchildren. I rest my case.

CHAPTER 23

Lust

Introduction:

I think that any writer should try to write about things that are morally clean. This kind if writing could also be called 'inspirational writing'. If I, as a writer want to have my work influenced by divine inspiration, It would be good for me to read the bible and learn what the revealed word of God has to say about sex and moral matters. Anyone can receive revelations through scriptures or through the mouths of prophets or through the 'whisperings of the Holy Ghost, who is the medium through which those messages will be sent, or affirmed. The Holy Ghost is the third part of the Godhead and because He is a Spirit and without a body, He actually has the ability to dwell inside us. Those revealed truths will be joyfully shared and will contain positive and pleasant and intelligent messages.

On the other hand, the Lord knows what we are thinking and He will know if we are actually in need of a <u>warning</u> instead of a series of best wishes. I think that the following essay will serve as a warning to everyone and especially to those men or women who find their carnal desires difficult to control.

I realize that <u>lust</u>, as opposed to healthy sex, is a filthy thing, and a bad thing to think about and even an unpleasant topic for a writer to write about. I only write about it here for two reasons and they both will come as warnings. One reason is that unbridled lust is probably the biggest destroyer of marriages and families that there is, and 2, because the modern media tries to normalize it whenever they can, IE: in music videos, advertising and movies. The producers of those wicked attempts at unrighteous persuasion will consistently play audiences for patsies and they will, most of the time, get away with it.

Women in pornographic videos may deserve pity, but in reality some of them are carnal people and have been compared to 'brute beasts' and end up, to use a scriptural term, on a brush pile, or to use a non-scriptural term, in a moral dustbin. No matter how much they doll themselves up or sharpen up their acting abilities, it seems that they have no allegiance to anything unless there is money or notoriety involved.

> *"But these, as natural brute beasts, made to be taken and destroyed, speak evil of the things that they understand not; and shall utterly <u>perish</u> in their own corruption."*
> *– 2 Peter 2: 12 (emphasis added)*

Most males who frequent those women in real life, or in their imaginations, are aware of this and they probably have very little feelings for those women. That can change though when a man gains a better knowledge of reality. To those men such women are pieces of meat or playthings and that is not what God intended for His children. As a result, few of those women can gain an honorable man's respect. Their disrespectful status has, unfortunately, already been established in his mind.

So what happens to a man when the man gets familiar with such women? He cannot have very much respect for them, or even possibly for any other woman, depending on how much exploitation he has allowed his imagination to stretch. It is sad, but true. Everybody makes mistakes and mistakes always have consequences, big ones or little ones.

Thus, it becomes difficult for a man like that to ever have a happy marriage with a decent woman. That is because he is, metaphorically, nothing more than a worker bee. He does his job. Makes his money (honey) and amuses himself by seeking cheap thrills for the rest of his lonely life.

That is the sad part. He did not know that his inner thoughts and desires could last through his earthly life and even extend into the realm that will be his next life. That next level might be heaven or hell or even one if <u>the three levels of glory</u> as they are explained in 1ˢᵗ Corinthians 15: 40-42. The highest kingdom of glory is called the Celestial Kingdom, or 'Heaven'. It is the one where our heavenly parents live. It is also the one that all people who desire a righteous final abode should strive for.

"There are also celestial bodies, and bodies Terrestial; but the glory of the Celestial is one, and the glory of the terrestrial is another. There is one glory of the sun, and another glory of the moon, and another glory of the stars: for one star differeth from another star in glory. So also is the resurrection of the dead."

– 1ˢᵗ Corinthians 15: 40 – 42 KJV

This is how the post mortal realm can generally look. In the Celestial kingdom a man needs a good and a faithful companion in order to feel fulfilled. It should be a companion who is trustworthy and dedicated. The same applies to a woman's needs. Her husband needs to be trustworthy and dedicated so that the both of them can reach the highest level of heaven and, by God's grace, abide there permanently. If that doesn't happen for us we must prepare ourselves to exist at a lower level, even one that is better suited for a single man or a single woman.

If a woman is physically beautiful, a normal carnal-minded man will usually seek physical gratification, or have 'lustful feelings' for her. The woman will know it and in the Celestial kingdom everyone else will know it too. This is because the Celestial Kingdom is a place where truth and knowledge are all around.

In the Celestial Kingdom, adultery and fornication are not allowed according to the laws of that kingdom. Therefore, a woman will not want to go to another level of heaven where the men there have hidden agendas and lustful desires. The women there will know who those men are and will not want to associate with them.

Therefore, logically speaking, a carnal-minded man will not be welcome there. Again, this will be, again, because the Celestial kingdom is a place where truth and knowledge abound. Women will not desire to go to there if they know there are men there with hidden agendas. Therefore, if a man goes to another level of heaven, there will probably be no beautiful women in that kingdom because the women there will be wise to all of their hidden agendas. Furthermore, if there are no beautiful woman in the place where a man goes after he dies, then he might ask himself if he is even in heaven at all.

Therefore, I say that it would be wise for people living in this mortal world to scrap any ideas of lusting after women or having hidden agendas in this world because those attitudes and behaviors can naturally carry over into the next world that they will occupy. Again, that principal applies to women as well. These principles also apply to homosexuals.

That is why I say that it is best for men and women to control their sexual appetites. If they cannot do that then a vision of the bigger picture will be what they need to grasp in their minds. If they still cannot do that, then <u>sincere 'repentance' in this world is the only safe way to find good companions or spouses</u> for the present or in the realms to come. This includes those realms that are of an Eternal nature. That is the reason that being faithful to your spouse is one of God's commandments. Thus, I say, let all men and women be absolutely honest in their romantic intentions at all times.

"THE GLORY OF GOD IS INTELLIGENCE."
– Doctrine and Covenants: 93: 36

"My God is an intelligent God. He is also a loving God and a happy God, even a joyful God. Thus, divine intelligence is necessary for gaining happiness and for having a purpose in life. I would therefore submit to you that the best kinds of intelligence and happiness come when you seek to do good and have a sure knowledge that love, with all of its facets, is being practiced in your home and in your life to the best of your ability.

It is also important for you to resist sin in whatever forms it may present itself. When you make effort to do these things, you will have the support and backing of millions of righteous people, righteous families, and devout Saints who have lived in this world throughout the history of it, and who will endure forever in the worlds to come, hopefully with <u>you</u> by their side."

- Reverend Bob

CHAPTER 24

Prayer

*"I always feel good when I counsel new people about prayer.
I think that I just might be introducing them to a wonderful
new Father that they never even knew they had."*

- Reverend Bob

In my deepest moments of peace, I am cognizant of the seriousness of life and I am also cognizant of mistakes I have made along the way that might have prevented me from ever receiving answers from Almighty God, a God who understands the necessity of thinking clearly. Fortunately, God is quick to forgive.

<u>In my deepest moments of peace,</u> I pray and ask my Heavenly Father to assist me in my healing. This is so that I will remember the intensity of my covenants and of my pleadings and of my sincerity. It is also so that both God and I will both remember the wonderful interaction that we had together in the past and will, hopefully, have together in the future.

Prayer is how we communicate with our God. It was that way from the beginning; that is, from the time of our first parents. Some people who have not incorporated prayer into their lives may not see a reason to do so. Perhaps they have tried it out and have not have received discernible answers to those prayers. This was the case with me when I first said a prayer. I perceived that there was 'nobody home', or so I thought. I do believe now though, that I was probably not asking the right questions, nor was I in the right frame of mind. I did not have a clear concept of what I should be asking and whom I was addressing. I also needed to know who was doing the asking. In other words, I needed to know who was I, as a person, and what were my exact wishes were. I realize now that I was not clear then on either of those points.

"Ye receive not because ye ask amiss."
- James 4:3

A double-minded person is a person who wants to find God and attain spiritual peace, and yet still has strong desires of the flesh and/ or seeks approval from other human beings. If this double- minded person asks God in prayer how to find happiness, which mind will God speak to?

I have been a double-minded person in the past. Many people, including some devout saints like St. Augustine in his younger years, have, by their own admission, been double-minded. They were people who sought righteous answers, but still had overpowering fleshly desires. In such cases, how could the Lord answer those prayers? His response, I would imagine, might be one that amounted to something like - 'no comment'.

If you are unfamiliar with the process of prayer, you should experiment with it. That is because, even though it does not always work when we ask amiss, it definitely can work when your life gets difficult for any reason and you are sincere about your desire for righteous change. So pray to your Father in heaven. He is the literal Father of your spirit. He wants you to be happy, He knows how you can achieve happiness and He is willing to assist you in that. So run to Him. Don't run to a part of yourself. It doesn't work when you try to be your own Father.

From my experience, answers to prayer usually come by feelings and promptings instead of words. Do not expect too much, but do not expect too little. It might take some pondering time to get an answer, but, personally, I find that, if the person praying is clear headed, the answer to their prayer can often come <u>in an instant</u>.

Prayer is much more than words. We might say a prayer in English or Spanish or Chinese, but that doesn't matter because it is the <u>feelings</u> that matter most. God understands languages, but He understands feelings better.

Prayer should come from the heart. Thus, any questions should be answered in the heart. God knows what each one of us needs, but here is no point in Him answering our prayers if we are incapable of receiving His answer.

Answers can come in words and I have experienced that, but from my from my experience it is rare. They usually come in a feeling or a prompting of some sort. A feeling of affirmation can just be a feeling of peace and knowing that something is right, or not. It could even be described as a feeling of 'good vibrations' or a 'burning in the bosom' or a clarification of thought. If an answer is negative, or if a question is unclear, an answer could come as a 'stupor of thought', as opposed to clarity of thought. Clarity of thought will come by the Holy Ghost. He knows our thoughts and can speak to us, when appropriate. He speaks in a 'still small voice', as was spoken of in the scriptures.

> *"and after the wind an earthquake; but the Lord was not in the earthquake: and after the earthquake a fire; but the Lord was not in the fire: and after the fire a still small voice"*
>
> *- 1 Kings 19: 11,12*

The point is that we need to be aware of the nature of the feelings that are being communicated to us. We need to enter into that same communication zone that the Holy Spirit is in. This may come with time and practice, but we will need to be spiritually in tune if it is to be a two-way interaction, which it should be.

Most of the time, God is not here on the earth to talk directly to us. That was part of the original deal. We live in a fallen world where God is somewhat distant from us and no one, as far as I know, has announced any changes to that status. Nevertheless, He has made it clear that there are ways to communicate with Him and sincere prayer is the main one.

There is a promise in the scriptures about the Holy Ghost who will "teach us all things and bring all things to our remembrance". (John 14:26). Prayer is how we connect with our God. It happens through the vehicle of the Holy Ghost who is capable of living inside us. Thus, it is impossible to keep secrets from Him.

When we pray, we should pray to God the Father, just as Jesus, who is our exemplar, did. We give thanks and then we ask for the things that we feel we need or things that someone else may need. We can give praise, but we always close our prayer in the name of Jesus who is the Mediator between God and man. Some people pray to Jesus, and I do not say that those sincere prayers will not be answered, but the correct process, as He taught us, should be to pray to the Father through the Holy Ghost and in the name of the Christ.

Can God answer the prayers of a Buddhist or a Muslim if Jesus is not mentioned? I believe those prayers can be answered to some extent if the prayer is given in humility, sincerity, and in righteousness. This is backed up by a scripture from Romans that says,

"Any sacrifice given in righteousness is acceptable to God."
- Romans 14:7

So it would appear that some prayers are given in righteousness and some are not. I mean, for example, that if a person who was a radical Muslim should pray for the death of all infidels, then I doubt very much that such a prayer would be answered, unless by an evil spirit. That is not a righteous prayer. The same would apply to a Christian or anyone else who asked for anything that was of an unrighteous ambition.

On the other hand, when we feel a righteous spirit, we will be better prepared to communicate with God. Sometimes a prayer might not be answered at all. That may be because we have not prepared ourselves fully to receive the answer with certainty. It would never be up to me to say if a prayer will be answered. It will always be up to Him in all His wisdom to give answers to prayers.

Perhaps we will need to have more immediate and personal questions answered first before we get our answers on other topics. For example, we might need to know something about ourselves before we know information about the things that are causing us anxiety or stress.

God is quick to forgive most sins. This is because He knows that we 'know not what we do' (Luke 23:34). But He also expects <u>more</u> from those of us who are more capable of having spiritual insights. He expects such people to learn of His ways and to keep on learning. The excuse of ignorance may, or may not, be acceptable, but I think that is something that has a definite time limit on it. He may deem it necessary for us to feel the pain of guilt for our misdeeds so that we might learn from them, but He may desire that we feel sorry about them for as little time as is needed. Thus, He is quick to forgive, but forgiveness must always be asked for because that is the only way to show Him that we actually desire it. Otherwise, if we do not ask for it, God could be seen as, sort of, 'meddling' in our affairs and He does not work that way.

The times when we feel guilty about something are the perfect times for the devil, or 'the accuser'; to try to get to us and convince us we are not worthy of receiving forgiveness or anything else from our righteous God. Our God does not want this to happen, so He is quick to forgive.

When we know this, and repent, it is easier for us to draw near to Him once more and continue to feel His Spirit. Still, even when we are forgiven we are still in the bottom part of the bubble and the repentance process needs to be followed through on. We may still have a ways to go upwards in the bubble before we are in full fellowship with Him. Nevertheless, He desires to keep us safe from evil forces, so that guilt will not cause our spirits to sink lower.

> *"Draw nigh to God, and he will draw nigh to you. Cleanse your hands, ye sinners; and purify your hearts, ye double minded."*
>
> *- James 4: 8*

God is close by. It is we who need Him. He does not need us. Therefore, we must seek Him out. The Holy Ghost, if He is present, will teach you what you need to know <u>at a particular time</u>. That topic of concern that you need to know about might be the furthest thing from <u>your</u> mind, but you must have faith that He is wiser than you are and He sees all things and all of the contexts of those things.

He knows that you should learn things, including learning things about yourself. Knowing those things might need to come in a certain order. Thus, the process of learning might be called 'holistic'. He may advise you to know things that you never asked for because those things may be vital to receiving a clear answer from Him.

When we talk to God, we should talk to him as we would to a loving Father and not a cruel one. He is our spiritual Father and He wants to be our Father. Thus, we should <u>allow</u> Him to be a Father. Some people put God in a difficult position. They sincerely want help from Him and ask for it, but they want it on their own terms. That is just not the way it works.

Prayer is like tuning in to a very fine radio frequency. We try various frequencies until we find the right one for us and then we keep our dial tuned to that place without letting it slip away as it is prone to do. Pray for however long it takes to gain the Spirit. If the time is right, a sincere ten-second prayer is better than an hour of just going through the motions. On the other hand, regarding important matters, we are advised to 'pour out our soul to God' *(Enos 1:9)*.

It is important to remember, while praying for help with our problems, that the Lord is <u>primary</u>. Our problems are important too, but because God is so important in all aspects of life, our personal problems become secondary. If we concentrate on the secondary problems, we need to remember that without God, the secondary factors will just build up and then crumble like a house of cards. God's order is what we must keep in mind and when we follow that order, He will then show us, in His way, everything we need to know.

Regarding intimate relationships, God has made it clear what the law is, that there should be no sexual relationships before, or outside of marriage. At some points in time a man and a wife might find their sexual compatibility out of sync. Should they pray about it? Definitely, but they should also talk frankly about it first, and try to pinpoint the problem and try to think of a 'higher solution' that is based upon truth.

In seeking the Lord's guidance in such matters people need to be very careful. That is because as I said, the Lord has His laws that are non-negotiable and there are good reasons for that. On the other hand, the devil is very familiar with sexual activity and there might be strong temptations brought on when people consider deviating from the ideal. Thus, people need to be aware of the dangers that might be lurking there in their minds.

In any case, this book is about my purpose in life so I should not be afraid to tiptoe around certain intimate issues. It is my main purpose to do the will of the Lord as best as I can. That is because when the Lord's blessings are not there, all other factors will eventually crumble.

Sexuality is an intimate thing and people will do what they will do, but we all have a choice as to what that will be. However, there can be some mistakes that we make. When there is mistake made the people concerned can discuss it frankly, decide on a solution, then move on. God is quick to forgive mistakes, but when people make a mistake, it is important that they acknowledge the 'no-fly zones' that comes along with their repentance.

Spiritually speaking, there is a haunted house somewhere in the consciousness mind, or the subconscious mind, of every person. It is an ugly thing and is positioned strategically in one's mind, and at the right time, by evil entities for the purpose of tormenting or tempting you.

That is intimidating because it is a very chaotic realm and it is also intimidating because of its sheer ugliness. Don't ever purposely go there. If you should stumble into that place accidentally, <u>ask God to make it vanish</u>. He has the power to do that. As well, He has the love for you to do that for you upon your request. This is assuming that you are strong willed enough to stand strong in following His word.

CHAPTER 25

Prudence

LIFE'S RAILWAY TO HEAVEN
"Life is like a mountain railway with an engineer that's brave.
You must make your run successful from the cradle to the grave.
Watch those hills, those curves and tunnels. Never falter, never fail.
Keep your hand upon the throttle and your eyes upon the rail.
Precious savior thou will guide us till we reach that blissful shore
Where the angels wait to join us in thy praise forever more."
- from a bluegrass song written by Charles D. Tillman. It was a variance on
an old hymn called 'Truth Reflects Upon Our Senses'.

This is an essay about prudence. I would personally define the word 'prudence' as the exercise of 'righteous caution'. This applies to driving a train or to many other things in life. This would also especially apply to principles of self-discipline and self-restraint.

Those are holy principles, but the word 'prudence' is something that is often neglected in the intellectual dissertations of certain intellectual or artistic principles. That is because that word is considered by nay Sayers to be freedom reducing or being too restrictive. Hence, the word 'prudish' is often used in its place. But that word has a negative connotation in many social circles. Let me be clear though that 'prudence' is actually a clean word and a 'dear' virtue and it has always historically fallen under the category of 'wisdom'.

More specifically, prudence is said to be simply the moral equivalent of being 'cautious'. Caution is considered a very underrated virtue in many quarters. This essay is a commentary on one of the most common struggles that most people have in life. What happens when we actually abandon that virtue of caution? I say that the results of that abandonment can often be devastating and sometimes even tragic.

The original idea behind caution, or prudence, is preservation. That is, the preservation of a virtue like chastity for example, or a virtue that is praiseworthy or the preservation of anything that is, or was, of great value. It could be the preservation of what might even be the preservation of a good relationship or a holy way if life. If such things are not worth fighting for then I would ask, 'what then is worth fighting for?'

Prudence might be occasionally associated with another virtue that we sometimes come across called 'righteous anger'. To believe in righteous anger means that there is actually some things are so important that they are actually worth a man or a woman 'fighting for'. 'Righteous anger' is a term that is dismissed by the pseudo intellectuals and leftists for the same reason that self-restraint and self-discipline is dismissed as being elitist. That is that it can be perceived as 'restricting our freedom to do what we want'. It is my opinion that such things are examples of 'calling good evil and calling evil good'.

In general, people can define a word or a phrase so that it means whatever those people want it to mean. That does not, however, make a certain definition right or valid. Virtue signaling implies that – "my definition is more fair or tolerant, and therefore I must be right and you must be wrong. "When virtue signaling is real, it can be 'fair game', but when it is used for manipulative purposes, it is a 'dirty strategy'.

If a person is accused of using righteous anger, the accuser is usually assuming that person is a hypocrite. They are saying that the person has a snobbish feeling of self-righteousness and they feel superior to most other people. That is another example of the twisting of words and definitions. It is a trap that some people fall into, but it is a lie that is always instigated by 'people manipulators'. Those manipulators feel that righteous anger is a bad thing because they say that people who claim to be righteous to so only for their own ego and their own greediness.

Left wingers, in general, say that religion itself is meaningless and that morality itself is evil because all moral judgments are relative and that people who say they are moral only say that to confirm their own superiority.

That is how words can be twisted around and therein lies the flaw. People who seek excuses to justify their behavior will push that point so that righteousness will be seen as merely a matter of opinion and therefore meaningless. For a person to say that righteousness is evil is only one example of a twisted mind at work.

Marxists state that Religion itself is nothing more than the 'opiate of the people'. In their eyes it all comes down to idealism and tolerance, which are the most common ways of dealing with crime without having to pass judgment and thus, avoiding minor judgments on one's self. They find it handy to see many serious issues as 'relative issues'. If you can convince a jury that there is really no such thing as a real crime and just see the perpetrator as a victim, that criminal will probably will get a pass, or a 'get out of jail free' card.

If there is really no such thing as malicious crime, then God or Jesus cannot become a judge in the affairs of man. They are just not tolerant enough. That is not part of the original deal however. Malicious evil is a sin and there must be a process that deals with that and that process would naturally involve punishment as a deterrent. Nevertheless, God will always be the FINAL JUDGE in the end and that IS part of the deal, a big part of it. He created the whole law making process and thus, He is in charge of it.

Righteous anger, or even righteousness itself, in the eyes of an ideologue, is just an opinion at best and a very flawed opinion. Flawed opinions can sometimes be deemed admissible in a court of law, especially if the judge himself, or herself, happens to be likewise flawed in their own thinking.

It will also be the judgment of left leaning journalists who consider themselves to be "paralegals' according to the unshakable 'laws' of political correctness. Those pseudo-journalists have invaded the world of legitimate journalism in recent years at an alarming rate. This is mostly as a result of the government or power brokers who literally 'finance the news'.

Members of the journalism community often have a penchant for believing in a twisted version of good and evil. They can see the merit of presenting a 'good excuse' and they may see it as something praiseworthy without ever realizing that that kind of justification is untrue to any journalistic ethics.

Thus, harmful and cruel behavior can be excusable or forgivable in a kangaroo court, instead of being seen as something that has evil at its core.

Thus, the judges and lawyers who have the power to 'get a person off' are often even more to blame for committing a 'miscarriage of justice' than the actual criminal who did the dirty deed. Career criminals are aware when the justice system goes off-track and it substantiates their philosophy that the world is 'dog-eat-dog' place. They will then proceed to preach that attitude to everyone they meet, either in blatant ways or subtle ways. That is actually how crime waves spread. It becomes acceptable to people without scruples.

The mind's inner workings say that a person's abandonment of caution has led them to be open to self-destructive forces setting their personal standards. If you think you can handle any problem with your great intelligence, take my word for it, you cannot. The devil knows how people's egos work and he laughs in their faces.

If the abandonment of caution that we aim for turns out to be nothing but a 'clown show', then such disgraceful schemes will eventually be exposed for what they are. That will be a shameful debacle and a true miscarriage of justice.

Just ask Joe Biden after he left thousands of American citizens and American allies alone in Afghanistan, what prudence and preservation, and loyalty means. He will not have an answer because those things are secondary to him. If you agree with his thinking then I say that you then you have not yet learned what you needed to learn in life, or even in politics. Thus, recklessness and chaos will prevail in your life as well as in the lives of other people, many of those people being innocent people. That means that you will have denied the virtue of prudence (or caution), which provides a degree of safety that, in the end is something that only wisdom, even divinely inspired wisdom, can provide.

It is a difficult journey at best, but especially when you have to try to get to an ethical conclusion of it all without any outside help. That is why I recommend a life of faith in our Redeemer and seeking the Divine assistance of the Holy Ghost who acts exclusively with the will of the Father. Thus, I only make one suggestion if a man or a woman has hit rock bottom. That suggestion is simply to 'let the Holy Spirit into your life'. Invite the Father, Son and Holy Ghost in. All three of those act as one, always. They have proven their qualifications a long time ago.

So here I am in Lumsden, Saskatchewan, Canada where I, as a humble ex-folksinger, hobble around in my personal quest of trying to live a decent and responsible life, but who still has to deal with bureaucratic bullies, who feel they are in control of every action that I choose to take. Still, I have faith that things will work out because I know that there are many good people in the world who have common sense and a desire to do what is right and even fight for that right.

They stand with me and so I know that I am not alone. I also have faith in a living God who is watching everything that happens to us. As well, I say that if we are obedient, He will often be prepared to 'step in' on our behalf when things go totally off the rails. I believe that the rewards of victory will go to the valiant followers of God who do not yield to the desires of the vile power seekers and bullies of the secular world.

As I lay out my personal thought patterns every day in my journey, those thought patterns would eventually trigger the true desires of my heart, for good or bad. I cannot honestly say that my desires have always been good, but they have always been my choice and I accept accountability for them.

Sometimes, I may have not done my duty perfectly and may yet be penalized for that. I may have even erred in my ways under a counterfeit banner of wisdom. Such wisdom is, sometimes, the wisdom of a fool, even a fool who has always been a pretty good 'banner maker'.

Honest and diligent workers who are faithful and true to Him will always carry out his instructions. The master of the vineyard, or the railway, knows who those workers are and He will rejoice when they make covenants to support Him in any way that they can.

After all is said and done, I say that the spiritual abandonment of caution and the replacement of it by things like pride, (including the pride that is alcohol driven) that will keep us away from our most precious destination, which is Eternal life itself in the Celestial kingdom.

Pride will never work even though there will be many men and women who will try to make it work. They will all fail in their efforts, even efforts that might be seen by them as somewhat valiant. In any case, that abandonment of caution will lead to the annihilation of every man and woman who decides to travel that route, and that will probably be brought on by their own actions.

> *"By the wicked are the wicked punished."*
> *- Mormon 4:5*

People need to be strong in this life and being humble before God is the best way to start gaining strength.

> *"And if men come unto me I will show unto them their weakness. I give unto men weakness that they may be humble; and my grace is sufficient for all men that humble themselves before me; for if they humble themselves before me, and have faith in me, then will I make weak things become strong unto them.*
>
> *– Ether 12:27 (The Book of Mormon)*

This, I humbly say, is the solution to our problems and it is the only solution to our problems. Be humble, be kind, be smart, and be prudent.

CHAPTER 26

A Marvelous Work
and a Wonder

When I was young, I used to get up in the morning and immediately my thoughts would go to 'all else', instead of meaningful things or even sacred things. I believe they call that 'the folly of youth'. I am thinking at this moment that in my everyday life, I've got to get back to thinking about things that are ultimately of ultimate importance and do so <u>to the exclusion of all else</u>.

Yes, I need to be more focused on the things that matter. I was always pretty good at the 'all else stuff'. I spent all my life at it trying to organize it and master it. It did not work out too well. I realize now it was a game, mostly a useless game of vanity. Sacred things are the things that matter now. Those are the things that last.

I would say that I have worked most of my life striving to master 'all else' and I too often ignored anything that required deep thinking, not because I was afraid of deep thinking, but I because I too often hit a barrier that prevented my thoughts from going further forward on the trail. As well, I didn't seem to have a lot of 'back up' along my way. My friends just weren't interested in the same things that I was interested in. It is not that daunting to think of sacred things. What is one example simple, but sacred thought. It is something that Jesus once said. Despite his gargantuan mission, he said:

"My yoke is easy and my burden is light."
- Matthew 11: 30

Was he taking His mission to save the world lightly? I think that he just valued the idea of simplicity.

"The Lord reasons in plainness and simplicity."
- Doctrine and covenants 133: 57

There are numerous thoughts that we might regard as sacred and that apply specifically to us, but will we expand on those thoughts or just dismiss them as being too simple, or even as unsolvable mysteries? Also, will we take notice of any special thoughts we have and record them in our minds and hearts and be able to bring them forward when we need them or expand on them on our private moments?

Books of scriptures, like the Bible and the Book of Mormon can provide many thoughts that are worthy of our contemplation. That is why they are there. And that is one reason why the Holy Ghost was sent to us. That is to provide us, on occasion, with a witness of the truth of the scriptures.

"But the comforter, which is the Holy Ghost, whom the Father will send in my name, he shall teach you all things and bring all things to your remembrance."
- John 14: 26

If you are stressed or grouchy when you arise in the morning, it is probably not because you are faced with sacred things. Your stress or grumpiness is probably because you are facing 'all else' and that may not be an exciting prospect.

God is not too interested in 'all else'. He has already figured it out, so He trusts that we too should be able to figure out that stuff on our own, but, hopefully, with some divine assistance if we ask for it. He is more interested in the salvation that comes to all of us when we follow the truth than interested in knowing how to get 'a few dollars more'. No matter how savvy one thinks they are, 'all else' can cause stress for anyone who subscribe to all of the challenges that 'all else' can bring to us. Instead, I say that we should present ourselves in spirit, to the Lord, and be mindful of a simple, but important, or even sacred thought that resonates within you. That thought might be that you are a child of God with a divine heritage. Another thought might be a simple one like the one quoted in John 3:16.

As we evaluate principles, we also evaluate behaviors and people. That is all right as long as our original impressions are not 'written in stone'. Evaluating people includes evaluating all kinds of people. Do I want to be a part of that Jungian cosmic consciousness where the spirits of 'all people' reside? No thanks. I would not want any part of the thinking process of a serial killer. Nevertheless, there are many people who we meet who are worthy of our thoughts. Everyone has their own story. Some stories may be worth listening to and some may not be. In any case, trust in your better judgment, or your 'higher self', as it is being guided by your own faith in the good.

Some people can think about nasty or unpleasant thoughts out of habit. Is a decades long habit difficult to displace? Yes. That is why it has been said we will be required to have a 'mighty change of heart". It will be a change that we must undertake on our own, and it will have a whole new 'thought zone' or time frame for it. It will have a new time frame because it will have a new starting point to it. That means that the new starting point will be in the present moment.

I seek revelation for my own sake, but if there is inherent wisdom in a revelation that I deem to benefit me, then it should be of benefit to others too. If you seek spiritual truth and revelation from the Holy Spirit, there is a good chance that you will receive it, but is truth always recognizable? No. It will only be recognizable to us after we become better acquainted with it.

A revelation from God does not need to be complicated.

> *"For my soul delighteth in plainness; for after this manner doth the Lord God work among the children of men. For the Lord God giveth light unto the understanding; for he speaketh unto men according to their language, unto their understanding."*
>
> *- 2 Nephi 31: 3 (Book Of Mormon)*

I went to a meeting once shortly after I became a member of my church. The meeting was held in a church that was not my own. It was billed as a meeting that would be an expose about the doctrine of the LDS church. I just wanted to check it out and see how the speaker could possibly twist the beautiful and intelligent doctrine of my church around so that the doctrine could be seen as evil, and even as Satanic, by an uninformed audience. I was quite shocked and disgusted by the speaker's efforts to do that.

The speaker went through his talk and he said some things that were innuendos and some were even bold faced lies, but mostly it was filled with 'half truths', or partial truths. That is, things that were partly true but could not be explained because which there was no one there from the church of Jesus Christ of Latter Day Saints who was invited to give a rebuttal or explain our views and beliefs, or to challenge the speakers accusations.

I had phoned the pastor of the church earlier and offered my services to explain some of the accusations that I knew would be brought out, but my offer was turned down. I asked the pastor if he thought it was fair that there should be such a one sided opinion delivered to his congregation. He could not, or would not, answer that question. He never did answer my question about 'fairness' and I could sense that he was a little embarrassed by that.

At one point in the meeting, the speaker began to rail about how my church was false because we did not utilize the symbol of the cross and how you would never see a cross on the top of a 'Mormon church'. I figured that the cross was, in reality, an instrument of torture and should not be exalted, but I kept quiet. There was another voice however that spoke out at that point.

It was a woman's voice. It was a very gentle voice and because it was dimly lit it seemed that no one could tell exactly what part of the building that voice was coming from. The woman called the speaker gently by his first name and said, "If Christ was killed with an electric chair, would you put an electric chair on the top of your church?"

The speaker was silent. He had no answer. I never did find out who the woman was who spoke that question.

There are some people who like to talk about the horrors that Jesus went through during His crucifixion and I have thought about those things myself at times, but I still say that when we contemplate the life of our savior we should not think too much about the blood that He spilled or the lashes he endured or the verbal abuse that was directed at Him, or the nails that pierced his hands and feet. I think that it is better to simply acknowledge the marvelous work that Jesus did as He sacrificed his physical body and endured lengthy torture for the sake of you and I, and who, in the end, even managed to ask for forgiveness from His Father for His cruel tormentors.

We need to recognize the courage that Jesus exhibited and the beauty of the offering that he gave to us, and once we do that, we should stay in that mental zone for awhile, so that we may contemplate that unimaginable sacrifice that He gave us. It was truly a marvelous work and a wonder. And that should be mostly what we should remember Him for. Our lingering in that zone should be enough for it to bring a confidence to you and me that will literally last us for the rest of our lives and beyond.

If we have errands to run or a business deal to complete or a hole in our roof that needs fixing, we can concentrate on those things, at various times, but the general **feeling** that drives us in our everyday actions should be one of gratitude for the great sacrifice that He made for us. That alone will give us the confidence that we need to endure to the end and also to give us a lingering feeling of personal happiness, or contentment, or even a joy that can last forever. Will God's kingdom last forever? Here is a quote from the Book of Daniel:

> *"And in the days of these kings shall the God of heaven set up a kingdom, which shall never be destroyed: and the kingdom shall not be left to other people, but it shall break in pieces, and consume all these kingdoms, and it shall stand for ever."*
> *- Daniel 2: 44*

CHAPTER 27

To Fight Or Not To Fight? That Is The Question.

SUBTITLES:
- Personal Relationships and Verbal Abuse
- Conformity
- Questions

One night I woke up out of a sound sleep at. It was 1:30 A. M. I was thinking that I needed something important to do, but I didn't really know what it was. My first thought was to check my bodily systems. Things seemed to be working all right, so it seems there must have been something else that I felt I needed to attend to.

I got up to have a drink of water and ended up watching Jordan Peterson and Rex Murphy, who is a Canadian journalist. They were having a discussion on You Tube. They were talking about current affairs in Canada. There was a lot of intellectualizing happening on the program, which was both good and bad. Some bad feelings were brought to mind because of a betrayal by the most prominent leader in the country, who happens to be the boy simpleton Justin Trudeau.

The reason why I thought that it was bordering on bad because the two of them really had no solution to offer as to how to rectify the problem that came when Justin enacted the emergency measures act in February of 2022. The discussion was good in another way though because it was very thorough and explained the conservative points of view very well, which was unusual on a television network that was 'state owned'.

The topic was important because it came lust after the news that Trudeau made one of his pious announcements that basically introduced the implementation of a fascist form of government to the Canadian people. He said that working truckers and people in other professions should be required by law to follow a mandate to take a basically untested vaccine for the Covid 19 pandemic.

That, the politicians said, was to help them in the fight against that disease that had been declared by medical 'experts' to be happening in the country and even in the world. Justin left no room for disagreement or discussion or individual choice, in the matter of taking the vaccine. It was his way or the highway. Take it or get out. Such a tyrannical attitude left the people without individual choice was not the mark of a good leader in the personal opinions of many.

The idea for an insurrection might seem to be the logical thing for citizens to consider, but I knew that they would probably not go there because then they would be seen as advocating violence. The idea that violence should be considered as an option was almost blasphemous in the politically correct version of the society that we lived in then. It was a very large taboo. All kinds of fierce accusations would fly from people if anyone spoke up in favor of a violent insurrection.

A fairly large union of truckers however had some problems with vaccine mandates and they organized a protest that consisted of a large convoy of trucks going to the capital city of Ottawa, which was a long ways away, and they 'hunkering down' there for awhile. The truckers knew about the deviousness of their political leaders and were aware that they needed to be careful about what they said and did in public, so they were cautious and law abiding.

Nevertheless, many of the truckers who were just present at the protest were actually arrested and many people who had donated money to the cause of the protesters had their bank accounts frozen by the government. I just could not fathom how a government in a free country that were allowed to freeze citizens private bank accounts just because the Prime Minister did not like their political opinions.

In short, it was a dark day for civil liberties and for the government and for the big banks, which had a mandate to protect the accounts of citizens. Those were citizens who took it for granted that the money they deposited into their accounts would be protected by the banks and by the people who worked there. The actions of the banks sucking up to the government was seen as an act of betrayal by many people, and rightfully so, in my personal opinion.

But was denying any thought of violence a good thing? There is not an easy answer to this. Many good people say that tyranny must be fought against or else that tyrannical behavior by the government would overcome the democratic principles of citizens, and as a result, their country might become divided and literally collapse. That idea did not seem right to me and to most freedom loving Canadians.

While watching that video, I thought of another post that I had seen on face book recently that stated another principle that was at work. The post began by showing a picture of a wolf in the wild. A wolf is a noble creature. There was a caption under the photo that read something like, "This is the difference between human beings and animals. A herd of animals would never choose the most feeble minded of the herd to be their leader, but a group of human beings would actually do that".

That meme made a lot of sense to me. In fact, I saw it as a universal truth. On contemplating this issue further, I thought the following thought – "The answers to the world's problems are always there, but another problem was that if the source of the information was a cheap television show like I had been watching, it would cause people to lose heart and just become apathetic about the matter. Thus, most people would not take that principle too seriously and would not see it as the 'freedom preserving' principle that it was.

Nevertheless, the principle that "All tyranny should be fought against and fiercely' was a worthwhile principle to think about. The idea could be thought provoking for both educated people and uneducated people.

I also had another thought come to me that said, this thought of never using violence would be totally accepted by many citizens today for the reason that most people are very afraid of violence, and for obvious reasons. In any case, it seemed to me that their fear of violence in Canadians was stronger than their love for freedom of choice.

In the Bible however, God allowed violence to take place many times and even on one occasion, he used it to wipe out almost all of the human beings (and animals) who lived on the face of the earth. I am talking here about people who were very active sinners and who were living on the earth around the time of Noah and his family. Those people became victims of a great flood that happened at that time according to the Bible. Most if the world's population and animals too, were drowned because of that flood.

The point is that the minds of most people, those who were mostly driven by culture as well as a love for security would not be in favor of using violence to take on a new way of life. The flood might have sounded too drastic as a punishment, but living a sinful way of life was a big part of those people's lives and God knew that their behavior would eventually bring destruction upon them anyways.

Thinking about social upheavals of all sorts, average people, including myself at times, would tend to think things like, 'Well, lets first see what a famous psychologist like Jordan Peterson might say." Or lets see what a famous actor or actress might think about this. Or "lets see what a famous musical pothead like Willy Nelson might think". Or lets see what a 'talking head' announcer from a billion dollar television station might think."

Those things are called 'distractions'. Distracting means taking the focus of men, women and children away from the important matters in life, like freedom, and putting focus on the icons of pop culture. Creating distractions and glorifying drama in the modern world are two things that television people have shown themselves to be very good at.

I assume that you see what I am talking about here. My point is that such an audience member who is constantly being lulled into a state of complacency is pretty much useless when the people cut themselves off from becoming active in a righteous, and even universal cause. In other words, I am saying that the correct answers are always there. The problem is that people will <u>not</u> normally 'receive' those answers into their heart and apply those answers to their lives so that good things can actually happen. Even the average citizen can be a contributor to that. That is when they become captivated by the fear of violence.

The Nephites in the Book of Mormon faced a situation like that. It looked like they were facing destruction from an enemy tribe when their leader came up with a novel idea. He fashioned a flag out some ragged remnants of cloth. The flag read – "IN MEMORY OF OUR GOD, OUR RELIGION, AND FREEDOM, AND OUR PEACE, OUR WIVES AND OUR CHILDREN."

This flag became known as 'THE TITLE OF LIBERTY'. The Nephites then prevailed in the ensuing battles and won the war.

Personal relationships and verbal abuse

'To fight or not to fight?' is an age old question and it applies to many things. In personal relationships tyranny can still exist when one person exercises dominance over another person. That could mean the male or the female in the relationship. Aside from physical violence, people who have the ability to use their words and personal insults with accuracy can be quite extreme in their nastiness and in their desire to control others.

Thus, I would advise anyone to never let another person, politician or not, take away their freedom and allow themselves to get lulled into a

Mindset of false security and choose to consent to a government mandate instead of valuing their own God given freedom of choice and their own independent ways of thinking.

People's natural instincts can be cruel and some people can be very adept at bringing another person into a state of submission by the sheer the nastiness of their words and their ability to 'pick on' the more vulnerable people who are near them. We should never, in any case, allow the more vicious people among us to abuse or take advantage of any peace loving people.

"Death and life are in the power of the tongue"
– Proverbs 18: 21

Another example of tyranny is for one person, who is part of a couple, to leave their partner who they dedicated themselves to because they did not want to face up to previous commitments they once made. I would not dare answer that question, but I know that it happens and it is always a sad thing when it does. There may be other reasons, but thankfully. I will not be the one to be the judge what ultimately happens in those instances.

"The genius of men and women is only exceeded by their ability for self justification and making up excuses."
– P. W. Doodle

Conformity

The tendency to conform to a mainstream point of view is not tyranny, but there are many things that are within that realm that can be used as weapons by bullies, male or female. I am talking about things like peer pressure, fear of being ostracized, and a fear to investigate a certain religious system that is questionable to onlookers and busybodies.

I have spoken in public many times in the past about political issues, because although it may get ugly, it is still important. Politicians today are making the laws that our children and grandchildren will be forced to live by. I don't know about you, but my children and my grandchildren are very important to me. They are not just the remnants of a bygone era. But when I talk about contentious issues, I find that a lot of people get bored and I can also find myself getting a little tongue-tied and perhaps even glassy eyed as well. But when I talk about God and Jesus I seem to come alive and I find that my words come easier and sometimes with passion. In those moments I find that I can actually reach certain people. An interesting conversation for me, is always one where the people involved seek out a solution for any problems that might come up. A conversation is never inspiring for me if a possible solution, and a positive one, is never mentioned. That is almost always a waste of my time.

I have had good conversations many times and the main reason for that is because, firstly, I know the scriptures and secondly, because I believe the scriptures. I also know that when I do give a good talk, I never expect any praise to come to me. If there is any praise that comes it should never come to me, but any credit I might receive should always be given to the God who orchestrates all important matters.

I studied the Book of Mormon when it was first given to me. The main reason that I studied it, at that time, was to find mistakes in it. I am still looking for those mistakes. In any case, the study of it was tremendously rewarding.

Questions

The main question I am asking in this political essay about 'fighting' essay is this:

Should ordinary citizens try to start a violent insurrection when the leader of that country tries to stifle freedom of speech and freedom of assembly and, as well, tries to bankrupt the country in the name of establishing a one world government that ignores traditional borders in the country that have been in place since it's founding over for a hundred and fifty years ago? Should a people invoke change jus for the sake of change?

I will leave the answer to those questions up to my readership.

Regarding joining the army during a war, I will say that if I lived in the U.S.A. and I had a son who was of fighting age, I would strongly discourage him from joining up and fighting if an incompetent man like Joe Biden was in charge of the military. Likewise, since I now live in Canada, I would give the same advice to my son if a feeble minded little boy like Justin Trudeau was in charge of making military decisions.

C H A P T E R   2 8

A Fighting Spirit (and gaining strength)

SUBTITLES:

➲ Bob's Obbs on gaining strength

> *"If your personal survival is what you want, a fighting spirit*
> *at the right time will be something you will eventually need."*
>
> *- Reverend Bob*

A fighting spirit is not always a negative thing. Last night, at the house of some friends, I, in my crippled up state, managed to throw a football to an eager six year old. Perhaps that was a minor fighting spirit I displayed, but it was a positive one for me and it was a highlight of my evening.

My point is that I hope that I will never lose my appreciation for youth and I know I will need to exert effort to do that. In it's own way that means I may need to fight, or just try harder to be active in the things that Iike to do.

I also know that I should never lose my appreciation for the creative writing that I do, or for the music that I make, or for anything that interests me. This applies especially to the interest I have in living and studying the gospel of Jesus Christ, which has the awesome power to bring about my redemption at the end of it all. I would add that it is my positive fighting spirit that will allows me to carry on that fight in my own ways and not give it up.

I will try not to ever entertain any thoughts of anger, covetousness or negativity into my mind. It is the positive fighting spirit and self-control that makes a person a whole person. It is even 'righteous rebellion' against our natural impulses that will prevent us from thinking negative thoughts.

> *"A drop of sweetness will probably roll down the ripe fruit of your life today my friend. Taste it. Enjoy it. Know that if something is good in your life then 'fight' to preserve that thing. Such will always be a good fight."*
> *– P.W. Doodle (From his book, 'How Sweet it is.)*

Choose life, not death, and not mediocrity. We usually have three choices. It is very easy for us to say, "I choose life" when things are going good for us. It is not so easy to say that when coercion or addictions or anxiety rear their ugly heads. Instead, we should actively be seeking out activities that allow us to feel that we are fulfilling a good purpose in our life.

To find the joy in living takes a strong mind, especially when things are not going your way. When we successfully do that we must take our righteous accomplishments to heart and embrace them with as much enthusiasm as we can. Right?

For example, if you are a singer who is singing a simple song, sing it with enthusiasm, from beginning to end. Be consistent. People will notice. Otherwise, you may need to compromise and settle for a 'lesser form of excellence', and, ipso facto, 'a lesser form of happiness', which, to those of us who feel the constant need to live at a higher level, is unacceptable.

It is a fighting spirit and a joyful one, by which a person can ruthlessly dispose of all carnal or obsessive thoughts from entering into your noble mind. It is a fighting spirit that encourages me to have self–restraint. Restraint is not when a person 'backs off in fear'. Restraint is when a person forges <u>ahead</u> with courage as they are in pursuit of a higher goal that requires perseverance. To restrain one's emotions we should sometimes rely on a 'fighting spirit', which is an admirable quality when it is mastered.

Restraint goes hand in hand with 'courage'. The courage I speak of is courage that is not just rehearsed. It is actually practiced every day in the world when we stand up for what is right.

Bob's Observations on gaining strength
(from my book, 'Life Goes On and On and On' by Reverend Bob.

If we do not have inner strength to begin with, we can always borrow it in order that we might try it out to see if we can handle it. Who can we borrow it from? We can borrow it from our Creators. Our Heavenly parents are quite willing to share their strength with us.

Test that strength therefore in the privacy of your own home. Our Heavenly parents possess much strength and it is a part of their parenthood to give strength to us when we need it and if we ask for it. Part of our earthly education is to learn what strength is, where it comes from, how it works, how we can develop it on our own, and how we can receive it from higher sources.

I am talking about trying to gain a balanced, or intelligent kind of strength here. I am not talking about a strength that shows itself in ferociousness or rage or cynicism. Those things are worldly views of what strength is. Displays of such things are displays of a false strength and do not work in the realms that matter the most.

Let us use Jesus as our example once again in the matter of finding strength through obedience. He did not ever say, "I can do this". His attitude during His entire mission was to be submissive to His Father's will and give all glory to our benevolent Father. We should do the same.

One part of strength is having clarity of thought and a singleness of mind. Keeping our thoughts simple can make us stronger rather than when we try to complicate matters and think too much. When we know who we are, our perception equation is in balance, that is, unless we become deceived. If some person, or force, should try to deceive us, we will more aware of those agents of deception when we have our minds on God, or on His Son, who are both eager to serve us.

In my life I have, at times, had control over certain circumstances, events and people in the secular world. I once saw these things as my strength. In fact, they are my weaknesses. My strength comes from what I call on from above me, not from below me.

Strength is best measured not so much by what we emit <u>out</u> of our bodies or our minds, but by what we refuse to allow <u>into</u> them. At first glance, the word 'strength' implies a strong will and a forceful, even tenacious, personality, but these traits can also apply to a stubborn mule who never listens to anyone else under any circumstances.

Young man, do you want to be a strong man? Then you must learn from people who are tough and strong. Who are they? They are the people who are the most self-disciplined. They know very well what it is like to 'go without'. They also know how to stand up for what is right.

Young woman, do you want to be strong? That is good. You will need strength, but please don't sacrifice your femininity for appearing to be strong. Can you have both strength and femininity? Absolutely, but it takes intelligence, cleanliness, dignity and will power. You have it in you.

Some people think that their ability to see their indulgences through to their conclusions is a sign of strength or power, but that power could be to rule over a Kingdom that amounts to nothing more than a small pile of horse manure on the Saskatchewan plains. Inner strength is not seeing indulgences through to their conclusion; I.E. going on a drinking binge.

True strength is having the power to restrain ourselves from indulging in such things in the first place.

Don't try to be too diverse. Be single minded in your righteous desires. Once you have established your point, walk away satisfied. The 'fragmentation' of a personality is the first step towards the disintegration of that personality.

We need to seek out our <u>spiritual reference points</u> every day and learn more about them. Just doing that will make us stronger. I would compare it to eating food that contains vitamins and minerals. We cannot physically see how vitamins and minerals make us strong, but we can see what happens when we do not have them in our diet. We slowly get sick. We become stronger spiritually when the 'vitamins' of the Spirit nourish us.

If you ask God to share His strength with you, He will do that and you will be blessed with strength, but He asks that you share His righteousness at the same time so that you will know what to do with that strength after you receive it. You do that simply by being obedient to His rules. When you are obedient to the commandments, you will find that you can actually see yourself, and feel yourself, getting stronger.

Lingering strength is maturity and maturity requires three things: knowledge of the truth, devotion to the truth, and articulation of the truth. To be articulate, people need to see the big picture. They also need to practice using words well every day and to come to know of their power and effectiveness.

People should use the best words they can and use those words as they apply to truthful principles, and then 'decide' when to use those words regularly. When someone uses those words wisely in his, or her, conversation, that conversation becomes a work of art instead of just rambling, or babbling about their opinions. They would be best to use the words of a wise mentor, one who has proven himself, or her self in the arena of debate.

C H A P T E R 29

How to Win an Argument

SUBTITLES:

- ➲ Clarity
- ➲ Blood on the Tracks

Arguments, disputations, bickering, contentions, dissent; such things have always been the cause of conflicts and upheavals among men and women, not only in nations, but in families and marriages too. So I ask now, 'What is the best was to resolve an argument, or even a pointed discussion, when two different sides of an issue cannot resolve their differences?'

Clarity

The best way that I have heard of to do that is to get each participant in the argument to state their view to the opposing arguer and do it to the satisfaction if that opposing arguer. Such would, theoretically bring clarity into the picture.

First of all, it is a true principal that when one tries to twist the meaning of what another person is saying, that is when the truth automatically goes out the window, and thus, resolution will not be possible. This is, to my understanding, a "misappropriation of justice'. Thus, it is the stealing of truth. Stealing is an immoral act. This can also be a problem when one person uses a MINOR example of an injustice and ignores a larger and a MAJOR example of an injustice.

One example of this is when protestors disrupt traffic, but the protesters claim they have a right to free speech, but the people who are stuck in their vehicles claim they have a right to 'freedom of movement'. Which one is right, or more right? What does a law enforcement officer say should be the priority?

One good way to resolve an argument is to get the arguers to 'agree to disagree'. This puts the higher principal of agreement ahead of the lower principal of disagreement for the sake of somebody's self-interest. I could also mean that having a right to a reasonable opinion is higher that proclaiming a flawed ideology or even just nit-picking.

A biased ideology is not a sensible way of debating. That is because the proclaimer of that ideology usually just assumes they are right and assumes that the vast majority of people think the same way that they do. This is a false way of thinking, but if an ideologue has been steeped in a certain way of thinking, then it is often difficult, or even impossible, to get through that impasse. Thus, that impasse can cause a 'misappropriation of justice' and a solution to the problem is going to be difficult to achieve.

Blood on the Tracks

People can agree to disagree, but one problem with that comes is when there is 'blood on the tracks'. That means that one person can be deeply offended by another person's allegations or insinuations. A discussion on the underlying problem can be beneficial, but can often be fruitless because, basically, some people are stubborn and 'set in their ways' and 'blood on the tracks' often just calls for retribution or for revenge in whatever way is handy.

That is why I personally, would seek for a spiritual solution to the problem. In other words, try to find the highest moral principal that you can and if you find one, use it to illustrate your point.

Jesus has been called the 'Prince of Peace'. From all accounts, He was a gentle person who always looked for the highest principles to live by. One example of that is the story of the 'woman taken in adultery'. In that story, the proof of the accusation of adultery was there and the mob wanted to stone the woman to death according to the law of the land. They knew that Jesus was a teacher and they respected Him, so they asked Him for His counsel.

Jesus pondered the matter for a while and then He drew a few pictures on the ground with a stick. I would imagine that He was trying to think of the perfect words to say. He eventually said,

"He that is without sin among you, let him first cast a stone at her." (John 8: 7)

The mob slowly disbursed until there was none left. Jesus asked the woman, "Woman, where are those thine accusers? Hath no man condemned thee?"

She said, "No man Lord." And Jesus said unto her, "Neither do I condemn thee: go, and sin no more. *(John 8: 11)*

This is one example of Jesus using a wise principal to supersede a lesser principle. He sought to do the will of the Father and, thus, do what would be the best decision of His own higher self. There are many examples like that in the New Testament.

As I said, sometimes there is 'blood on the tracks' when the wound has cut deep. When Jesus was crucified He was first accused of blaspheming against God, which was a very serious sin among the Jews.

The hurt then, or the 'blood', could not be allowed to go away. The sin was not to be forgiven according to the Pharisees, and Jesus, who was the Savior of the world, was then crucified to death by a mob because the Pharisees, or the priests, demanded it in the name if their traditional ways.

We all know now that that was a misappropriation of justice, even one that had been prophesied earlier in the Old Testament, but I figure that that was where there was an important lesson that needed to be to be learned, and learned not only by the Jews, but by the whole world. If they were wise people, they should have known that that is the way of the world without God. And that will be what needs to be remedied first.

Justice can only be returned to the world when the world will 'allow' it to return. When that it is countered by centuries of tradition, then it will be no easy task to change people's way of thinking. The alternative is to have society run by tyrants and dictators. That also includes mobs that use 'group think', peer pressure, and 'political correctness'. Those will usually be the main vehicles for various 'misappropriations of justice'.

C H A P T E R   3 0

Demons and Pornography

N o, I'm not trying to frighten you. Demons are real. 'There must be opposition in all things', even the most righteous things. Demons like to project pornographic images on people's minds, people who are vulnerable to such things. They do that and do it especially during a time when outside worldly stimuli are spurring such images on. We presently live in such a time.

At certain times some people can become filthy minded. They may not mean to be filthy, but an inclination to be that way makes them careless people to say the least. That is a serious fault in the case of pornography. Evil spirits are cognizant. The power of evil spirits is not strong, but in the right circumstances I.E: entertaining a vulnerable, or unprincipled mind, it is strong enough to break through barriers and hit people hard, even envelope them further in carnal thoughts and images that are particular to their lives and to their memory banks.

If your life has been shattered in some way, demons will know that and they will seek to reconstruct your life according to their own plan. They have the resources that they will need to carry out that plan. Satan has a very large resource section in his library.

There is only one answer to this assault when it and if it should come upon you. Replace your shattered-ness with a restoration. You will need to find a <u>new</u> purpose. Replace a part-time love of wrong-doing for a full time love of the gospel, including a love for beautiful new ideas and beautiful words. Read every day and pray that you might feel the power of the scriptures and the power of Christ. That's it.

Scripture study should become our most worthy pastime. Scriptures, believe it or not, are anti porn. They have amazing the power to rearrange a person's priorities when that person becomes willing to accept truth, pure truth.

When I get up in the morning, my thoughts should go to sacred things, even simple sacred things, instead of going to 'all else'. I have worked all my life striving to organize and master 'all else'. It did not work out well. It is not that daunting to think of sacred things. Whatever you are lacking, the Spirit will enable you to access great resources. They are resources that many brave people have laid down their lives so that YOU might benefit from reading them.

Often change will be <u>desired in us</u>, but there will come a time when change is <u>demanded in us</u>. That could be a time when we reach the point where we begin to hate ourselves because we realize the full extent of our personal weakness. There is no worse feeling than the feeling that comes upon you when you realize that you hate yourself because you realize that you have a serious personal weakness or fault.

You will need to be strong, even ferocious, when you are presented with things that endorse your weakness. That includes wicked imaginings by some outside influence.

Righteous anger is not a bad thing. My words to an evil entity on discovering it, "What are you doing here? You don't belong in my realm. Get out."

If you should ever see a pornography scene in the media, consider this, it is sad to see one who is in a state of innocence debauched, whether it is consensual or not. That scene could become a <u>permanent memory</u> in your mind if you are a witness of it.

Do you want that? That young woman, whoever she may be, could desire to return to her innocent state one day. She may desperately seek forgiveness for her sins. If your mind lasts forever, as I have stated elsewhere, your explicit memory of her and her doings, could go on forever too. You will therefore, not be able to forgive, and ipso facto, you will not be able to be forgiven either.

If the sex act was consensual at the time, that doesn't matter. If you are holding on to that memory you are, in a way, refusing to grant her forgiveness and thus refusing to allow her a new future. In a way then, you are still complicit in the act. Is that really something you want to do?

I am saying that a person can disregard the immorality of witnessing a sinful act because it was consensual, but a sin is still a sin. By memorizing the details of that sin and keeping it locked in your memory banks that can easily cause you to become complicit in it again.

I will need to focus everyday on who I am, – the good and final version of who I am, and who my God is. I should never focus on ego driven things.

The gospel is true. The Bible is a record of a people's spiritual history and is basically true. The book of Mormon is also a historical history and it is also true. How fortunate I am to have discovered this hidden knowledge. How dare I neglect the spiritual history of the world's spiritual people?

Who am I TODAY? Not fifty years ago or thirty years ago. What is important to me TODAY. And if I have to think about that too much, then I don't really know the answer. I will remain in ignorance and a state of carelessness. Accurate awareness can come in an instant or it can come over time. If it has to be mulled over for a long time, it is probably not awareness at all. It is probably unresolved analysis. Don't curse the world because you cannot resolve it. Get to work and resolve it. Awareness is resolved analysis, not unresolved analysis. They are two different things.

I want to be clear. I want to be clean. I am a man who loves God. I love Jesus and the Holy Ghost. This is because I have studied it and I have a testimony of the truth.

I always defend my family, unless they betray me. I defend my faith. I defend the truth and I do not put up with lies. I have enlisted in the cause of Christ to fight against the devil and his lies. I love most of the people I know and I try to serve them with good humor. Most of the time, I love my life, and I will testify that goodness exists. That is who I am, or at least, who I try to be. The Lord wants the best from His disciples. If I don't match up to that, I should drop out. As half a man I am doing Him no favors in enlisting in His cause. I should leave those things to someone else.

Pornography is poison. It just is. Trying to explain why is self-defeating. It always makes you feel afterwards that you have violated moral standards in some way. There are no excuses when you indulge in pornography.

If you are on 'the Apex of righteousness' through your diligence and your righteous faith in the good, then stay where you are. You are the King of the castle. The dirty rascal, however, is constantly sneaking up on you grabbing for your leg and with all his strength, is trying to drag you down. Be aware of his presence and don't let him do it.

The words of an old hymn is coming into my mind. It says, "I Stand all Amazed at the love Jesus offers me". I believe that God will not let the lives of any of his children go adrift without giving them at least one experience of love in their own life time.

I never thought that I was the kneeling kind, but knowing about the amazing things that He did for me, I would not hesitate to kneel at His feet. But there is more to it than receiving the gifts I speak of. You don't get something for nothing in this life, not physically, mentally, or emotionally. When the time comes to sacrifice your bliss lines or pleasure lines, for lines of 'duty', you should gratefully do so. That is your obligation according to the law of the harvest – we reap what we sow. As we are given light and love as gifts, we have a duty to give something similar back. If you feel that you are not given any light and love, I can only say that you need to look further into that issue.

Why do people crave to have a desire to control other people? ONE REASON. As I have said elsewhere in this book, it is because they mistakenly see personal control as a God like power that they can obtain. In fact, they cannot obtain it. Why not? ONE REASON.

It is because all things have their opposite and BECAUSE GOD HAS GRACIOUSLY GIVEN ALL HUMAN BEINGS THEIR FREEDOM OF CHOICE.

CHAPTER 31

Triumph

SUBTITLES:
- ⮑ Social Media
- ⮑ The Vines that Entangle Us

March 12, 2022

Face the delightful sunrise or the brutal jungle of your early morning meditations with pure honesty. Be unafraid to repent and be unafraid to be honest.

Meditation time: It is intense this morning as I try to bring my feelings and thoughts and memories into line with my higher self. I do believe in the power of prayer and that God will answer our prayers, but I also believe that He will often answer our prayers in His own way. He does this not according to what we say we want, but according to what He knows we need. He will also answer our prayers, perhaps not in words, but He will answer them in His own way.

> *"And it shall come to pass in the last days, saith God, that*
> *I will pour out my spirit upon all flesh and your sons and*
> *your daughters shall prophesy and your young men shall see*
> *visions and your old men will dream dreams."*
>
> *– Acts 2:17*

In a spiritual sense, I feel that I have a well-sharpened machete in my possession. I must bring that machete along with me as I travel through the jungle that is life. I must swing it fervently so that I can cut away the vines that are the lies and the confusing messages and the half truths that come onto my path and entangle me when I am facing the multitude of twisted vines that originated from the ignorance of my past. Vines are natural things, but that does not mean that they are good things.

I don't know if it was a dream or a vision, but last night I felt that I was walking through a dense and dark jungle. I knew that those vines that hampered my progress were harmful things. They contained the harmful and confusing messages that had been entering into my mind for several years. Such vines may come from academia or from government edicts, or from peers with half baked ideas, or from social media, etc.

Social media

I have seen a number of intelligent posts on face book, but I have also seen some false posts and some filthy posts that are embarrassing to witness. The biggest problem with that is that social media is very elitist. There is a subliminal hash tag that goes along with each post. It says, **'We are the experts and we say that this post is legitimate. It is proper and we approve of it. So take our word for it. We are the ones who know right from wrong.'**

Red flag. You should always be aware that people who offer half-truths to other people are, in the end, liars. And they should never be trusted.

The vines that entangle us

Those vines tend to wrap around my arms and legs and even my mind. They bind me. It may be easy sometimes to cut the lifelines of those vines that wrap around me with my machete, but at other times they can be difficult to cut.

This morning I felt that a message was being sent to me. I felt that it was a true message and it was literally above all the other messages that I was dealing with. It just had that positive resonance about it. So I wrenched myself out of my bed and I began to write. I don't know if God would ever instruct me by using the word 'fight', but I knew for certain that those vines that held me bound would need to be cut out and cast away.

I would advise people who suffer from anxiety, like me, to confess that state when it is present in their life. If the guiding hand of God seems to be absent, then admit your inadequacies and your disappointments and ask for help from above.

I say that all people should confess their absolute need for self-control and self-discipline in all of the things that they do. A person, and especially one who has had a complicated past, cannot survive without self-discipline. They cannot survive because of the many tentacled monsters from the past and even from the present that haunt them. Each tentacle, or vine, has its own demonic agenda. So get out of bed and write about it. More ideas will come to you as you practice self-expression and you will find that your mind will become noticeably clearer.

Don't try to change the things in your life that you cannot change. Some things are out of our control. That is life. Accept the serenity that comes with that knowledge and then have the courage to <u>focus on changing the things that you can change</u>.

Cut those vines that bind you. Cut them in half with your machete. Swing your machete with confidence and rhythm and, at times, with ferocity. Some vines have a tough fiber, but in reality they are just mindless organisms and when you cut off their lifelines they will just fall on the ground and rot.

Their growth is constant though. Growing and stealing nourishment from the roots of other plants is what they do. That is all they know how to do. Thus, you must swing your machete at them every day when they appear. After you cut them down then you can take a well-deserved rest knowing that your personal living space has expanded in righteousness.

I did that this morning and I had a good feeling about it all, might even describe it as a victorious feeling. My intellect was finally in tune with my higher self, which always includes spiritual promptings or feelings that have their origins that come from a higher place. Another word I might use for that feeling is **TRIUMPHANT.**

I held on to that triumphant feeling for as long as I could. The reason why I did that is because it felt good inside. **It is a goal of mine to feel good inside.** It is also a goal of mine to feel good inside about feeling good inside.

I wanted to remember that experience because I knew that I might not be so blessed on my next visit to the jungle. I wanted to remember the triumph that I felt at that time and I wanted to remember the serenity and the good feeling that I felt when my journey through the jungle was over, at least for the time being.

CHAPTER 32

Repentance

(IN A RELIGIOUS AND A NON-RELIGIOUS SENSE)

Non-religious people are usually intimidated by the word 're-pentance'. When I was younger, I, too, was intimidated by the word because I associated it with some street preachers in my neighborhood. Those street preachers were always mocked by the youth who I sometimes associated with. But I know now that the word 'repentance' is not to be feared and it would be a mistake to reject that word because it encompasses a valuable part of life that is essential to a person's progression or self- improvement. The word 'repentance' simply means to 'rethink' or to 'refocus'. If that is not already a standard mode of operation on occasion for a human being, I humbly say that it should be.

The whole purpose of self-improvement is based upon change and 'rethinking'. It is discarding old behaviors and old ways of thinking that have proven to be unfruitful in favor of newer notions that are more likely to make a person a happier person, and even a better person all around. Thus, the word should never be feared because it represents opportunities for learning and personal growth. Whether you are religious or not, that is just plain logic, even common sense.

Can a person 'repent' outside of the context of religion or Christianity? Using a general definition of the word, I would say, 'yes'. Anyone can instigate 'change'. In a religious context, the answer might be different. Sometimes a religious change might actually mean something if great importance, like **'a mighty change of heart'**.

In any case, if you should find the word 'repentance' alarming or threatening, I will give you a simple, short exercise to follow that might help alleviate some of your apprehension. First, I want you to think of something foolish that you did at some time in your life. Don't dwell upon it, but just think about what it was and if you still harbor any regrets about it. I suspect that everybody has something in their lives that they regret doing if only for the simple reason that none of us are perfect.

Okay. When you think of that thing that you regret doing, repeat these words in your mind – "I repent of that." Now, say it out loud – "I repent of that." There. Was that so hard? I do this just to get you to use the word once and realize that it is a good descriptive word that might be of use to you in your life. So don't be afraid of it.

Are you a person who now, or at some point in your life, was filled with too much pride or egoism? Most of us have been there at some time. Did your behavior at that time ever cause you to leave a bad impression with someone else or even do some harm to another person.

Here is another word that you might be afraid to face up to. The word is 'forgiveness'. If you can identify with accepting the word 'repentance' as a good thing, then why not try to make a clean slate of it all by accepting another important word. That word is 'forgive'. Similarly, think of a past situation or event where you unintentionally hurt someone and then say the words – "I hope that they forgive me for that." There. You have now become slightly more familiar with another important life skill. If you cannot think of a time that you ever hurt someone then I will honestly congratulate you for being an exceptional person, (or I might secretly wonder if you have a problem with telling the truth.)

But I will take you at your word however, so…'congratulations'.

I am quite serious about these exercises because I have met people, mostly from secular backgrounds who are mistrustful, or even deathly afraid of religious language like 'repentance' or 'forgiveness' because certain words call them to accountability, and some people have a private policy that prevents them from accepting any outside authority that does that.

It is human to make mistakes and there is no shame in it. The only way to erase those mistakes is to become familiar with redemptive principles like forgiveness and repentance. Both of those words imply 'beginning again with a clean slate'. WOW! I must exclaim. I am personally very thankful to have those opportunities.

Those principle are a part of an eternal plan and without an eternal plan, you have, basically, no plan. If a person is not familiar with those two redemptive processes, then they should be recognized as people who have no interest in correcting themselves when they make mistakes. Does that sound like you? Or does that sound like the kind of friend that you would want to have?

Plus, people who cannot 'change' will be setting themselves up to be <u>trapped</u> inside a deep hole, a hole in which freedom and peace of mind will be out of reach. I say that if a person does that they will be denying the spiritual side of existence and thus, cutting themselves off from the most important part of life, the part that can actually allow us to start over every single day of our lives.

A man who I regard as a prophet of God stated recently that we should get into the habit of repenting <u>every day</u>. Some people might reasonably wonder why they should do that every day when they might not feel that they have done anything that is really that bad. I maintain however, that it is a fact that <u>we live in a tainted world,</u> and because we live in that tainted world, it stands to reason that we might be a little bit tainted ourselves. We may not know exactly where the source of that 'taint' is coming from, but we know that it is there. If that is so, then I see it as a <u>great gift</u> that we can cover all the bases and simply repent every day and then start off each day with a clean slate.

> *"O that I were an angel and could cry repentance unto every people."*
>
> *– Mosiah 29: 1*

CHAPTER 33

Avoiding Temptations Through Music

SUBTITLES:

- ➲ Hymns
- ➲ Mississippi John Hurt
- ➲ Dion DeMucci

I have been going to church for over thirty years now and I have learned many hymns during that time. Someone once advised me to think of a hymn when I was tempted by something and then sing it to myself. It was good advice and I have followed that advice many times. The hymns are special songs. They are songs of worship and songs of gratitude. The words are enough to touch a person's heart and mind and remind them of the wisdom of God's plan.

The melodies of the hymns combined with the words, are often enough to touch a person's soul and remind them of God's love for His children. Many of the hymns could be regarded as scriptures in themselves, like How Firm a Foundation' or 'I Know That My Redeemer Lives'.

There are hundreds of hymns to choose from, all of them were written by talented, meticulous and faithful composers and lyricists. Take your pick as to which one you might want to use to heighten good spiritual feelings in your life.

Mississippi John Hurt

I heard a song when I was about nineteen years old. It was sung by an old black man named Mississippi John Hurt. He played an old guitar to accompany himself, and did so very well. The song had a pleasant melody and had a good and steady rhythm to it.

The words of the song were probably the most important part of the song for me. That is because it had a good message to it and it was it was a very motivating message. It repeated that message often, so that we could remember it as we were caught up in the melody and the rhythm of the song.

It even reminded people that there are some things that we <u>need to remember</u> because they will that keep us close to our noble mission, if we should claim a mission like that. I am sure that Mr. Hurt must have been familiar with the traps that come with temptations

The song was called, 'I Shall Not Be Moved' and here is one verse:

> *"On my way to heaven. I shall not be moved.*
> *On my way to heaven. I shall not be moved.*
> *Just like a tree planted by the water, I shall not be moved."*

The rest of the verses are pretty much identical musically. Lyrically, there are a few words changed around in the other verses. It is a simple song, but that is a good thing. The song is similar to a chant with the music repeating itself. Repetition can be good in a song. One reason for that is that the words are easy to remember for the singer. Another reason is that it is a way of continuing to 'be strong' in the message. In this case that is to avoid temptation, just like that tree that was planted by the water.

Dion DiMucci

Lately I have been revisiting an old hero of mine on the internet. His name is Dionne DiMucci and he had a string of hits back in the late fifties and early sixties, songs like 'Runaround Sue', 'Ruby Baby', 'Teenager in Love', The Wanderer', and many more. He started out as a doo-wop singer with his vocal group 'the Belmonts' on the streets of New York City. He was the lead singer in that group.

As of this year (2022), I believe he is eighty two years old. He married his high school sweetheart and the marriage lasted for his lifetime. Dionne is a one-man library of Rock and Roll history. He not only played music with the famous stars of his era, but he became close friends with many of them and he talks about them with fondness and with a first hand knowledge of the music of the time.

Although I have never met him, it seems to me there are many things that he and I have in common. Even though the level of 'stardom' that he reached was far greater than any level I ever reached, we both played the guitar, sang, and composed music. On a personal level, Dion played around with drugs and alcohol during his early years and I had similar experiences. Dion had a religious conversion when he was, roughly, in his early twenties. I also had my own conversion to Christianity, but that did not come to me until I was in my early forties.

The things that brought the gospel home to us both were almost identical. It came down to having a special witness of the truth. He is still a practicing Christian today in the Catholic Church. I am also a practicing Christian in the Church of Jesus Christ of Latter Day Saints. That conversion made a big difference in my life, and I gather from his you-tube interviews that it has made a huge difference in his life too.

When I listen to his descriptions of his religious experiences I am amazed at how powerful it was and how we are so similar in our thinking about God and about how religion in general works, even though there are many things that can be difficult to understand for some people.

Dion, it seemed to me, mostly faded out of sight in pop music when the sixties ended. That was partly because of the British invasion and the changes that were happening in pop music at that time. Dion did record a song called 'Abraham, Martin and John' around 1969. It was a song written by John Holler about prominent figures that had been killed by assassin's bullets, namely Abraham Lincoln, Martin Luther King, and John F. Kennedy.

It was a beautiful song and went to the top of the charts, but It did not seem to elevate Dion very much as a major 'star'. I figured that the reason for that was because the 'word was out' that Dion was a born again Christian and that was a 'taboo' in the world of pop music.

Born again Christians, it seems to me, just do not fit into what Joni Mitchell described as 'the star making machinery behind the popular song'. In any case, I still felt that Dion deserved to be among the top icons of pop music generally at that time and even of Rock and Roll specifically.

It is often the testimonies of other people that keep us active in a good cause and strengthen our faith generally in the powers of heaven. Dion's testimony was, and is, a great inspiration to me. That is why I include him in this section of the book on good spiritual influences and spiritual mentors whose ideas and talents can help any person resist the temptations of the lower self.

If you listen to him speak in his videos, he is so honest and articulate, even in a street-wise kind of way, that I am sure that you will be impressed by his perceptions and his sincerity about how to keep your faith strong and survive, and even prosper, in this difficult world.

Perhaps his words resonate with me because I am a musician, even one who has made a number of personal mistakes like Dion once did.

That also gives me the advantage that I know that Dion is telling me the truth. I know that he has been there and done that, and thus, I actually trust what he says implicitly. I love the testimony that he shares with all people and, wherever he may be today, I want to thank him for that.

I do not regard Dion as a prophet, but I am only saying that through his great faith, he was able to 'tap into' the creativity of the Universal God and, as a sideline, tap into the creativity of some of the great musicians and performers of his era and explain their talent very well and in a very human way.

Dion had a large part in the history of popular music. He was scheduled to be on that fatal trip to Fargo, North Dakota, the one that took the lives of Buddy Holly, the Big Bopper and Ritchie Valens in the late fifties. Dion was an admirer of others on the tour like the J. P. Richardson, ('The Big Bopper' and Ritchie Valens. Ritchie was feeling ill on that tour so Dion gave him his ticket to fly on the ill fated plane.

Dion tells of that incident, a few years later, when with the best if intentions, he gave his ticket to the young Mexican singer. Dion went through a phase where he suffered from much guilt because of his well-intentioned offer.

I very much admired Ritchie Valens when I was young after hearing his songs played on my old transistor radio. He was a great singer. He could take simple three chord songs like 'La Bamba' or 'Come On Lets Go' and with his sheer talent bring out a special magic in those songs.

J.P. Richardson was also an amazing talent. As 'The Big Bopper' he recorded a very unique song called 'Chantilly Lace' which had a driving beat to it and a unique style. Many years later, I was surprised to learn that J. P. Richardson also actually wrote a famous country music classic sung by the late George Jones called 'White Lightnin'.

My point here is that all a person needs to do is carve out a place for himself or herself in an activity that they have a certain amount of passion for. That should be enough to keep a person on the 'strait and narrow path'. That was Dion's experience.

The third performer who died in that crash in a snowy field was Buddy Holly. Buddy was a legendary singer and songwriter who had a string of hits, too numerous to name. It was even more tragic because he was recently married at the time died.

Listening to Dion's interviews, I strongly believe that a study of the gospel will serve you well and be of a benefit to you until the end of your days, as it was for Dion DiMucci, and maybe even for his ill fated companions.

Thus, you could find yourself pleasantly enveloped in a righteous and fascinating activity, along with other like-minded people. If you work hard and stay humble, as Jesus instructed us to, that should be enough to keep your own creative juices flowing freely.

C H A P T E R   3 4

Life Attracts Life and Spirit Attracts Spirit

In the second edition of my book 'Realms I Have Known', there is a true story about a man named Fred. That was not his real name though. His real name was Adam.

He died because of a neurological disease after his brain started to disintegrate slowly. I was not familiar with the demise of a human brain, but it was never something that I wanted to think too much about. I was also unfamiliar with the healthy workings of the human brain, even though many doctors, scientists, neurologists, researchers, and a variety of people are active in the study of the brain and how it works in conjunction with the body. I only knew that it usually worked pretty good for me, with perhaps a few flaws that I discovered over time.

Adam was very prolific speaker and functioned well in his life, and in his job and in his extra-curricular activities, and as a husband and the father of five children. I talked with Adam before he died and I asked him how he was getting along in the midst of his many brain surgeries. He confided in me that he did not feel that his brain was that much use to him anymore. He said that most of his thinking cane through his mind and his spirit. I assumed that that <u>also</u> meant the ultimate Spirit, which is called the Holy Spirit, which can actually live within us because (He) is the third part of the Godhead.

Of a certainty I would say that very little is actually known about the brain even in the medical profession. Despite the advancements in medicine the brain still presents many mysteries to many doctors. That is partly because the brain is encased within a hard, bony skull that protects the brain from physical danger. That is, perhaps, a good thing, but it also prevents us from doing too much 'peering' into that intricate organ to see exactly how it works and how it works in various situations.

In short, I would say that we lack information insofar as knowing the exact workings of the brain, even though qualified doctors are not without effort in this matter. That is confusing to scientists because the human skull is difficult to analyze because of the protective bones and membranes around the brain. Thus, the human brain is still beset with mysteries, despite any progress in the field of neurology or 'brain science'.

Nevertheless, I wonder how we can circumscribe all the uncertainty in neuroscience and try to explain certain possibilities about how the brain can work after our bodies die. The simple answer to that is that the brain doesn't work any more. That is the end of that story. It's all over.

Because of that, many living people can develop a sense of hopelessness about their very lives. That is not good and we all need a certain amount of faith to counteract that. There is also an alternative way of thinking that is backed up in a relatively obscure scripture. It is from a book called 'The Pearl of Great Price'. It is a part of the canonized scripture of the Church of Jesus Christ of Latter Day Saints. It states:

> *"The Lord created all things spiritually before He created them physically."*
>
> *- (Moses 3:5)*

This means to me that the creation of the 'mind' and the 'spirit' came before the creation of the brain. This means that we can actually 'think' in our spirits and/or in our minds as well as our brains. Ancient Greek philosophers like Plato and Aristotle talked about the actual cognitive abilities of our eternal minds and spirits many centuries ago.

Personally, I have had some spiritual experiences in my life, ones that I cannot deny, and reinforce some confidence that I have in human beings to think, even after our bodies fail us or even die.

I do believe that a powerful and all-knowing Creator would be capable of finding a way to <u>preserve</u> our character and personalities in whatever casing that our thoughts and ideas come from. Do our ideas, our beliefs, our memories, our affections turn to dust once the human heart turns off the switch? No, I say that my God is a greater God than that. The God that I just described I would call a 'puny God' and my God is not that.

My God set out from the beginning to get the job done and that is what He has done and that is what He will do in the future. That ability that He put into us makes us cognizant and aware now and even beyond the grave. Yes, I do believe that we human beings are much more that our brains alone.

Another reason for my thinking is that the human mind is connected to the human will. The brain alone cannot understand the human will. The mind, can somehow understand it. As a result of that, our preferred values will become will become a part of our will and a part of the values that we hold dear. That will be the source of all of the important decisions that we make in our lives. Yes, our 'will' is probably the driving force behind all of our decisions for good or bad.

Also, I suspect that our human mind also has a connection to our 'soul'. The soul is the God-given part of us that preserves both the 'feelings' and the 'cognition' that I spoke about earlier. That also has to do with our self-image, which is usually a wonderful thing, but on occasion, mischievous and wicked entities can tamper with it and disrupt its noble purpose.

The mind may be indestructible, but it is also delicate and vulnerable when it is left out in the 'natural elements' for too long. Because it is indestructible by nature though, it is also eternal.

How that actually works, I don't know exactly and I don't think that any doctors or scientists know either. It is out of their pay scale. Because of that, I have a suspicion that it is actually better that we know very little about the soul except for the fact that it actually exists. I actually fear that it might be dangerous for us if we knew too much. The Lord watches out for His children in His own way. Also, it has been said, that 'a little bit of knowledge is dangerous'.

And so I ask, is there something that can be present in our lives that we can become aware of and will give us confidence to know that there is a way whereby the good things in life can be preserved and even allow the continuation of our perceptions to some extent even after death?

The only answer to that, in my mind is that there is, what might be called, a very durable 'entity' made out of what we call 'Spirit' or even 'mind' that exists within our being.

"With God all things are possible."
- Matthew 26: 19

I quoted the scripture where it says God created our spirits before he created our bodies (brains) and thus, I think that <u>we learned to think with our spirits and our minds, 'before we learned to think with our brains</u>'. Therefore, in the next life I believe that we will be able to 'think' with either our minds or our spirits or both, and after some practice, do so fairly easily.

Because our bodies were entering into a physical world when we were born, we forgot about thinking with our spirit like we did in the pre-existence, and we begin to think in physical terms, or 'brain terms'.

This can be exciting for us as young children, because of the new adventure we begin to experience at birth. But there seems to be a problem though because we learn to forget many of the simpler things of the spirit, which includes feeling things like love and joy and peace that we experienced during the pre-existence.

We may be reminded of our spiritual side from time to time in life, but usually not enough to cause those spiritual things to linger and become a strong part of us. This can change over time though as we will have much time to spirit-think in the afterworld. It is all part of a new learning process, and that learning, or relearning process can be a 'difficult' one. Nevertheless, that will be all we have at that time, so I suspect that we just may adapt to it fairly quickly.

I realize that this idea might be difficult for some people to fathom; nevertheless I am sticking to it. That is because I do believe that the spiritual way of thinking is a higher way of thinking than the physical way of thinking. I also believe that that is the way that God thinks too.

> *"His ways are not our ways."*
> *– Isaiah 55: 8,9*

I think that God would partake of that spiritual way of thinking and even ask us, who are His spiritual children, to partake if it as well. That is because it would allow for all of us to partake of Everlasting things and do so in the Spirit as we make use of our resurrected bodies and our everlasting minds. The independence of our minds, or if you will, our spirits, will allow us to perpetuate the power of perpetual motion. That is sustained by the power of righteousness, love, and intelligence, which is in essence, the power of God.

Thus, I would also say that this idea of perpetual motion, or Eternal life, has been sanctified by the glorious resurrection of Jesus Christ, who is the only begotten of Son of God. I also say that we humans should not only embrace the wise laws that God has given us, but we should cherish them.

God's Spirit will always attract our Spirit and His life will always attract our life, as long as we follow the spiritual rules (the commandments). Going back to the title of the book, this is my purpose in life: To make our spiritual nature become clear to us all, and to influence others to let that influence to be the factor that will determine our personal Eternal happiness and, as well, our Eternal wisdom.

CHAPTER 35

The Second Coming

Christ said that He would come again to the Earth a second time in His resurrected body to complete the full restoration of the gospel. That will be the most tremendous event of all time, and I personally look forward to that glorious day.

I find that my words are not qualified to properly express my feelings on that so I will not even try. My allegiance in this life is not based on any philosophy or country or state or province or school. My allegiance is based only on Jesus Christ despite my unworthiness. I love Him. He is my guiding light. He is the savior of the whole world and WAS ORDAINED FROM THE BEGINNING TO BE SO.

Nevertheless, for now, we human beings are still in a mortal state until the end comes and we must have a strategy to cope with earthly adversity until that final end comes. It is important that we are able to show our love for Jesus during these end times. How can we do that?

Jesus gave us the answer to that question in His own simple way. He said that we could show our love for Him by 'obeying the commandments'.

"If you love me, keep my commandments."
– John 14: 15

So what then are the commandments? They are the laws of God.

If the missionaries went out to strangers out on the street and said, 'If you want to be successful in life, keep the laws of God', that might be well and good, but those words alone would probably not be enough to persuade anyone to believe in God and the reason for that is because, according to my personal observations that most people, not all, but most, DON'T REALLY UNDERSTAND WHO GOD IS, and as well, THEY DON'T UNDERSTAND WHAT HIS LAWS ARE. I say that they have never been taught those things, at least, not taught properly.

And that is where our 'work' comes in. The saints (disciples) are, or should be, 'teachers'. As teachers, <u>we</u> first need to know, as best as we can, who God is and what his laws are, and then we need to know the best way to express those things to others. That takes a lot of study and contemplation. Missionaries really do have a huge job when they go out into the world. They have their work cut out for them.

A lot of God's laws have been given to us in scriptures, but I think that there are laws that many of us just know instinctively by the Spirit, although certain people, by their own freedom of choice, can still choose to ignore those laws.

One of those laws that we can feel by the Spirit is to simply to treat everyone we meet with respect. That includes men and women, old and young, rich and poor, educated and uneducated, etc. If we can do that instinctively and <u>live</u> such laws with confidence, we can be successful. Not only that, the whole process of loving Christ and loving our fellow men and women will then become much easier for us, and more enjoyable as well.

Thus, He inferred that we should learn what His wise laws are and keep them, then He will take care of the rest. It is that simple.

I will end this book by getting back to the original question, which is, "What is my purpose in life? Thus, I would like to offer a short quote:

> *"Wherefore; be faithful; stand in the office which I have appointed unto you; succor the weak, lift up the hands that hang down, and strengthen the feeble knees. And if thou art faithful until the end thou shalt have a crown if immortality, and eternal life in the mansions which I have prepared in the house of my Father."*
>
> *– Doctrine and Covenants 81: 5,6*